THE WAY TO GOD

AND HOW TO FIND IT

THE WAY TO GOD

AND HOW TO FIND IT

BY

D. L. MOODY

ISBN: 978-93-5128-954-8(PB)

First Published in 1884
Indian Reprint in 2017

Published by

Kalpaz Publications
C-30, Satyawati Nagar,
Delhi – 110052
E-mail: kalpaz@hotmail.com
Website: kalpazpublications.com
Ph.: +91-9212142040

CONTENTS.

THE WAY TO GOD.

CHAPTER I.

"*LOVE THAT PASSETH KNOWLEDGE.*"

"To know the love of Christ which passeth knowledge."
(EPHESIANS iii. 19.)

IF I could only make men understand the real meaning of the words of the apostle John—"GOD IS LOVE," I would take that single text, and would go up and down the world proclaiming this glorious truth. If you can convince a man that you love him you have won his heart. If we really make people believe that God loves them, how we should find them crowding into the kingdom of heaven! The trouble is that men think God hates them; and so they are all the time running away from Him.

We built a church in Chicago some years ago; and were very anxious to teach the people the love of God. We thought if we could not preach it into their hearts we would try and burn it in; so we put right over the pulpit in gas-jets these words—GOD IS LOVE. A man going along the streets one night glanced through the door, and saw the text. He was a poor prodigal. As he passed on he thought to himself, "'God is Love!' No! He does not love me; for I am a poor miserable sinner." He tried to get rid of the text; but it seemed to stand out right before him in letters of fire. He went on a little further; then turned round, went back, and went into the meeting. He did not hear the sermon; but the words of that short text had got deeply lodged in his heart, and that was enough. It is of little account what men say, if the Word of God only gets an entrance into the sinner's heart. He staid after the first meeting was over; and I found him there weeping like a child. As I unfolded the Scriptures and told him how God had loved him all the time, although he had wandered so far away, and how God was waiting to receive him and forgive him, the light of the Gospel broke into his mind, and he went away rejoicing.

There is nothing in this world that men prize so much as they do Love. Show me a person who has no one to care for or love him, and I will show you one of the most wretched beings on the face of the earth. Why do people commit suicide? Very often it is because this thought steals in upon them—that no one loves them; and they would rather die than live.

I know of no truth in the whole Bible that ought to come home to us with such power and tenderness as that of the Love of God; and there is no truth in the Bible that Satan would so much like to blot out. For more than six thousand years he has been trying to persuade men that God does not love them. He succeeded in making our first parents believe this lie; and he too often succeeds with their children.

The idea that God does not love us often comes from false teaching. Mothers make a mistake in teaching children that God does not love them when they do wrong; but only when they do right. That is not taught in Scripture. *You* do not teach your children that when they do wrong you hate them. Their wrong-doing does not change your love to hate; if it did, you would change your love a great many times. Because your child is fretful, or has committed some act of disobedience, you do not cast him out as though he did not belong to you! No! he is still your child; and you love him. And if men have gone astray from God it does not follow that He hates *them*. It is the sin that He hates.

I believe the reason why a great many people think God does not love them is because they are measuring God by their own small rule, from their own standpoint. We love men as long as we consider them worthy of our love; when they are not we cast them off. It is not so with God. There is a vast difference between human love and Divine love.

In Ephesians iii. 18, we are told of the breadth, and length, and depth, and height, of God's love. Many of us think we know something of God's love; but centuries hence we shall admit we have never found out much about it. Columbus discovered America; but what did he know about its great lakes, rivers, forests, and the Mississippi Valley? He died, without knowing much about what he had discovered. So, many of us have discovered something of the love of God; but there are heights, depths and lengths of it we do not know. That Love is a great ocean; and we require to plunge into it before we really know anything of it. It is said of a Roman Catholic Archbishop of Paris, that when he was thrown into prison and condemned to be shot, a little while before he was led out to die, he saw a window in his cell in the shape of a cross. Upon the top of the cross he wrote "height," at the bottom "depth," and at the end of each arm "length." He had experienced the truth conveyed in the hymn—

> "When I survey the wondrous Cross,
> On which the Prince of Glory died."

When we wish to know the love of God we should go to Calvary. Can we look upon that scene, and say God did not love us? That cross speaks of the love of God. Greater love never has been taught than that which the cross teaches. What prompted God to give up Christ?—what prompted Christ to die?—if it were not love? "Greater love hath no man than this, that a man lay down his life for his friends." Christ laid down His life for His enemies; Christ laid down His life for His murderers; Christ laid down His life for them that hated Him; and the spirit of the cross, the spirit of Calvary, is love. When they were mocking Him and deriding Him, what did He say? "Father, forgive them, for they know not what they do." That is love. He did not call down fire from heaven to consume them; there was nothing but love in His heart.

If you study the Bible you will find that the love of God is *unchangeable.* Many who loved you at one time have perhaps grown cold in their affection, and turned away from you: it may be that their love is changed to hatred. It is not so with God. It is recorded of Jesus Christ, just when He was about to be parted from His disciples and led away to Calvary, that: "having loved His own which were in the world, He loved them unto the end" (John xiii. 1). He knew that one of His disciples would betray Him; yet He loved Judas. He knew that another disciple would deny Him, and swear that he never knew Him; and yet He loved Peter. It was the love which Christ had for Peter that broke his heart, and brought him back in penitence to the feet of his Lord. For three years Jesus had been with the disciples trying to teach them His love, not only by His life and words, but by His works. And, on the night of His betrayal, He takes a basin of water, girds Himself with a towel, and taking the place of a servant, washes their feet; He wanted to convince them of His unchanging love.

There is no portion of Scripture I read so often as John xiv; and there is none that is more sweet to me. I never tire of reading it. Hear what our Lord says, as He pours out His heart to His Disciples: "At that day ye shall know that I am in My Father, and ye in Me, and I in you. He that hath My commandments, and keepeth them, he it is that loveth Me: and *he that loveth Me shall be loved by My Father*" (xiv. 20, 21). Think of the great God who created heaven and earth loving you and me! . . . "If a man love Me, he will keep My words; and My Father will love him; and We will come unto him, and make Our abode with him" (*v.* 23).

Would to God that our puny minds could grasp this great truth, that the Father and the Son so love us that They desire to come and abide with us. Not to tarry for a night, but to come and *abide* in our hearts.

We have another passage more wonderful still in John xvii. 23. "I in them, and thou in Me, that they may be made perfect in one; and that the world may know that Thou hast sent Me, *and hast loved them as Thou hast loved Me.*" I think that is one of the most remarkable sayings that ever fell from the lips of Jesus Christ. There is no reason why the Father should not love him. He was obedient unto death; He never transgressed the Father's law, or turned aside from the path of perfect obedience by one hair's breadth. It is very different with us; and yet, notwithstanding all our rebellion and foolishness, He says that if we are trusting in Christ, the Father loves us as He loves the Son. Marvellous love! Wonderful love! That God can possibly love us as He loves His own Son seems too good to be true. Yet that is the teaching of Jesus Christ.

It is hard to make a sinner believe in this unchangeable love of God. When a man has wandered away from God he thinks that God hates him. We must make a distinction between sin and the sinner. God loves the sinner; but he hates the sin. He hates sin, because it mars human life. It is just because God loves the sinner that He hates sin.

God's love is not only unchangeable, but *unfailing*. In Isaiah xlix. 15, 16 we read: "Can a woman forget her sucking child that she should not have compassion on the son of her womb? yea, they may forget; yet will I not forget thee. Behold I have graven thee upon the palms of My hands; thy walls are continually before Me."

Now the strongest human love that we know of is a *mother's love.* Many things will separate a man from his wife. A father may turn his back on his child; brothers and sisters may become inveterate enemies; husbands may desert their wives; wives, their husbands. But a mother's love endures through all. In good repute, in bad repute, in the face of the world's condemnation, a mother loves on, and hopes that her child may turn from his evil ways and repent. She remembers the infant smiles, the merry laugh of childhood, the promise of youth; and she can never be brought to think him unworthy. Death cannot quench a mother's love; it is stronger than death.

You have seen a mother watching over her sick child. How willingly she would take the disease into her own body if she could thus relieve her child! Week after week she will keep watch; she will let no one else take care of that sick child.

A friend of mine, some time ago, was visiting in a beautiful home where he met a number of friends. After they had all gone away, having left something behind, he went back to get it. There he found the lady of the house, a wealthy lady, sitting behind a poor fellow who looked like a tramp. *He was her own son.* Like the prodigal, he had wandered far away: yet the mother said, "This is my boy; I love him still." Take a mother with nine or ten children, if one goes astray, she seems to love that one more than any of the rest.

A leading minister in the state of New York once told me of a father who was a very bad character. The mother did all she could to prevent the contamination of the boy; but the influence of the father was stronger, and he led his son into all kinds of sin until the lad became one of the worst of criminals. He committed murder, and was put on his trial. All through the trial, the widowed mother (for the father had died) sat in the court. When the witnesses testified against the boy it seemed to hurt the mother much more than the son. When he was found guilty and sentenced to die, every one else feeling the justice of the verdict, seemed satisfied at the result. But the mother's love never faltered. She begged for a reprieve; but that was denied. After the execution she craved for the body; and this also was refused. According to custom, it was buried in the prison yard. A little while afterwards the mother herself died; but, before she was taken away, she expressed a desire to be buried by the side of her boy. She was not ashamed of being known as the mother of a murderer.

The story is told of a young woman in Scotland, who left her home, and became an outcast in Glasgow. Her mother sought her far and wide, but in vain. At last, she caused her picture to be hung upon the walls of the Midnight Mission rooms, where abandoned women resorted. Many gave the picture a passing glance. One lingered by the picture. It is the same dear face that looked down upon her in her childhood. She has not forgotten nor cast off her sinning child; or her picture would never have been hung upon those walls. The lips seemed to open, and whisper, "Come home; I forgive you, and love you still." The poor girl sank down overwhelmed with her feelings. She was the prodigal daughter. The sight of her mother's face had broken her heart. She became truly penitent for her sins, and with a heart full of sorrow and shame, returned to her forsaken home; and mother and daughter were once more united.

But let me tell you that no mother's love is to be compared with the love of God; it does not measure the height or the depth of God's love. No mother in this world ever loved her child as God loves you and me. Think of the love that God must have had when He gave His Son to die for the world. I used to think a good deal more of Christ than I did of the Father. Somehow or other I had the idea that God was a stern judge; that Christ came between me and God, and appeased the anger of God. But after I became a father, and for years had an only son, as I looked at my boy I thought of the Father giving His Son to die; and it seemed to me as if it required more love for the Father to give His Son than for the Son to die. Oh, the love that God must have had for the world when He gave His Son to die for it! "God so loved the world, that He gave His only begotten Son, that whosoever believeth in Him should not perish, but have everlasting life" (John iii, 16). I have never been able to preach from that text. I have often thought I would; but it is so high that I can never climb to its height; I have just quoted it and passed on. Who can fathom the depth of those words: "God *so* loved the world?" We can never scale the heights of His love or fathom its depths. Paul prayed that he might know the height, the depth, the length, and the breadth, of the love of God; but it was past his finding out. It "passeth knowledge" (Eph. iii. 19).

Nothing speaks to us of the love of God, like the cross of Christ. Come with me to Calvary, and look upon the Son of God as He hangs there. Can you hear that piercing cry from His dying lips: "Father, forgive them; for they know not what they do!" and say that He does not love you? "Greater love hath no man than this, that a man lay down his life for his friends" (John xv. 13). But Jesus Christ laid down His life *for his enemies.*

Another thought is this: He loved us long before we ever thought of Him. The idea that he does not love us until we first love Him is not to be found in Scripture. In 1 John iv. 10, it is written: "Herein is love, not that we loved God, but that He loved us, and sent His Son to be the propitiation for our sins." He loved us before we ever thought of loving Him. You loved your children before they knew anything about your love. And so, long before we ever thought of God, we were in His thoughts.

What brought the prodigal home? It was the thought that his father loved him. Suppose the news had reached him that he was cast off, and that his father did not care for him any more, would he have gone back? Never! But the thought dawned upon him that his father loved him still: so he rose up, and went back to his home. Dear reader, the love of the Father ought to bring us back to Him. It was Adam's calamity and sin that revealed God's love. When Adam fell God came down and dealt in mercy with him. If any one is lost it will not be because God does not love him: it will be because he has resisted the love of God.

What will make Heaven attractive? Is it the pearly gates or the golden streets? No. Heaven will be attractive, because there we shall behold Him who loved us so much as to give His only-begotten Son to die for us. What makes home attractive? Is it the beautiful furniture and stately rooms? No; some homes with all these are like whited sepulchres. In Brooklyn a mother was dying; and it was necessary to take her child from her, because the little child could not understand the nature of the sickness, and disturbed her mother. Every night the child sobbed herself to sleep in a neighbor's house, because she wanted to go back to her mother's; but the mother grew worse, and they could not take the child home. At last the mother died; and after her death they thought it best not to let the child see her dead mother in her coffin. After the burial the child ran into one room crying "Mamma! mamma!" and then into another crying "Mamma! mamma!" and so went over the whole house: and when the little creature failed to find that loved one she cried to be taken back to the neighbors. So what makes heaven attractive is the thought that we shall see Christ who has loved us and given Himself for us.

If you ask me why God should love us, I cannot tell. I suppose it is because He is a true Father. It is His nature to love; just as it is the nature of the sun to shine. He wants you to share in that love. Do not let unbelief keep you away from Him. Do not think that, because you are a sinner, God does not love you, or care for you. He does! He wants to save you and bless you.

"When we were yet without strength, in due time Christ died for the ungodly" (Rom. v. 6). Is that not enough to convince you that He loves you? He would not have died for you if He had not loved you. Is your heart so hard that you can brace yourself up against His love, and spurn and despise it? You *can* do it; but it will be at your peril.

I can imagine some saying to themselves, "Yes, we believe that God loves us, if we love Him; we believe that God loves the pure and the holy." Let me say, my friend, not only does God love the pure and the holy: He also loves the ungodly. "God commendeth His love toward us, in that, *while we were yet sinners*, Christ died for us" (Rom. v. 8). God sent him to die for the sins of the whole world. If you belong to the world, then you have part and lot in this love that has been exhibited in the cross of Christ.

There is a passage in Revelation (i. 5.) which I think a great deal of—"Unto Him that loved us, and washed us." It might be thought that God would first wash us, and then love us. But no, He first loved us. About eight years ago the whole country was intensely excited about Charlie Ross, a child of four years old, who was stolen. Two men in a gig asked him and an elder brother if they wanted some candy. They then drove away with the younger boy, leaving the elder one. For many years a search has been made in every State and territory. Men have been over to Great Britain, France, and Germany, and have hunted in vain for the child. The mother still lives in the hope that she will see her long lost Charlie. I never remember the whole country to have been so much agitated about any event unless it was the assassination of President Garfield. Well, suppose the mother of Charlie Ross were in some meeting; and that while the preacher was speaking, she happened to look down amongst the audience and see her long lost son. Suppose that he was poor, dirty and ragged, shoeless and coatless, what would she do? Would she wait till he was washed and decently clothed before she would acknowledge him? No, she would get off the platform at once, rush towards him and take him in her arms. After that she would cleanse and clothe him. So it is with God. He loved us, and washed us. I can imagine one saying, "If God loves me, why does He not make me good?" God wants sons and daughters in heaven; He does not want machines or slaves. He could break our stubborn hearts, but He wants to draw us towards Himself by the cords of love.

He wanted you to sit down with Him at the marriage supper of the Lamb; to wash you, and make you whiter than snow. He wants you to walk with Him the crystal pavement of yonder blissful world. He wants to adopt you into His family; and to make you a son or a daughter of heaven. Will you trample His love under your feet? or will you, this hour, give yourself to Him?

When our terrible civil war was going on, a mother received the news that her boy had been wounded in the battle of the Wilderness. She took the first train, and started for her boy, although the order had gone forth from the War Department that no more women should be admitted within the lines. But a mother's love knows nothing about orders;

so she managed by tears and entreaties to get through the lines to the Wilderness. At last she found the hospital where her boy was. Then she went to the doctor and she said: "Will you let me go to the ward and nurse my boy?"

The doctor said: "I have just got your boy to sleep; he is in a very critical state; and I am afraid if you wake him up the excitement will be so great that it will carry him off. You had better wait awhile, and remain without until I tell him that you have come, and break the news gradually to him." The mother looked into the doctor's face and said: "Doctor, supposing my boy does not wake up, and I should never see him alive! Let me go and sit down by his side; I won't speak to him." "If you will not speak to him you may do so," said the doctor.

She crept to the cot and looked into the face of her boy. How she had longed to look at him! How her eyes seemed to be feasting as she gazed upon his countenance! When she got near enough she could not keep her hands off; she laid that tender, loving hand upon his brow. The moment the hand touched the forehead of her boy, he, without opening his eyes, cried out: "Mother, you have come!" He knew the touch of that loving hand. There was love and sympathy in it.

Ah, sinner, if you feel the loving touch of Jesus you will recognize it; it is so full of tenderness. The world may treat you unkindly; but Christ never will. You will never have a better Friend in this world. What you need is—to come to-day to Him. Let His loving arm be underneath you; let His loving hand be about you; and He will hold you with mighty power. He will keep you, and fill that heart of yours with His tenderness and love.

I can imagine some of you saying, "How shall I go to Him?" Why, just as you would go to your mother. Have you done your mother a great injury and a great wrong? If so, you go to her and you say, "Mother, I want you to forgive me." Treat Christ in the same way. Go to Him to-day and tell Him that you have not loved Him, that you have not treated Him right; confess you sins, and see how quickly He will bless you.

I am reminded of another incident—that of a boy who had been tried by court-martial and ordered to be shot. The hearts of the father and mother were broken when they heard the news. In that home was a little girl. She had read the life of Abraham Lincoln, and she said: "Now, if Abraham Lincoln knew how my father and mother loved their boy, he would not let my brother be shot." She wanted her father to go to Washington to plead for his boy. But the father said: "No; there is no use; the law must take its course. They have refused to pardon one or two who have been sentenced by that court-martial, and an order has gone forth that the President is not going to interfere again; if a man has been sentenced by court-martial he must suffer the consequences." That father and mother had not faith to believe that their boy might be pardoned.

But the little girl was strong in hope; she got on the train away up in Vermont, and started off to Washington. When she reached the White House the soldiers refused to let her in; but she told her pitiful story, and they allowed her to pass. When she got to the Secretary's room, where the President's private secretary was, he refused to allow her to enter the private office of the President. But the little girl told her story, and it touched the heart of the private secretary; so he passed her in. As she went into Abraham Lincoln's room, there were United States senators, generals, governors and leading politicians, who were there about important business about the war; but the President happened to see that child standing at his door. He wanted to know what she wanted, and she went right to him and told her story in her own language. He was a father, and the great tears trickled down Abraham Lincoln's cheeks. He wrote a dispatch and sent it to the army to have that boy sent to Washington at once. When he arrived, the President pardoned him, gave him thirty days' furlough, and sent him home with the little girl to cheer the hearts of the father and mother.

Do you want to know how to go to Christ? Go just as that little girl went to Abraham Lincoln. It may be possible that you have a dark story to tell. Tell it all out; keep nothing back. If Abraham Lincoln had compassion on that little girl, heard her petition and answered it, do you think the Lord Jesus will not hear your prayer? Do you think that Abraham Lincoln, or any man that ever lived on earth, had as much compassion as Christ? No! He will be touched when no one else will; He will have mercy when no one else will; He will have pity when no one else will. If you will go right to Him, confessing your sin and your need, He will save you.

A few years ago a man left England and went to America. He was an Englishman; but he was naturalized, and so became an American citizen. After a few years he felt restless and dissatisfied, and went to Cuba; and after he had been in Cuba a little while civil war broke out there; it was in 1867; and this man was arrested by the Spanish government as a spy. He was tried by court-martial, found guilty and ordered to be shot. The whole trial was conducted in the Spanish language, and the poor man did not know what was going on. When they told him the verdict, that he was found guilty and had been condemned to be shot, he sent to the American Consul and the English Consul, and laid the whole case before them, proving his innocence and claiming protection. They examined the case, and found that this man whom the Spanish officers had condemned to be shot was perfectly innocent; they went to the Spanish General and said, "Look here, this man whom you have condemned to death is an innocent man; he is not guilty." But the Spanish General said, "He has been tried by our law; he has been found guilty; he must die." There was no electric cable; and these men could not consult with their governments.

The morning came on which the man was to be executed. He was brought out sitting on his coffin in a cart, and drawn to the place where he was to be executed. A grave was dug. They took the coffin out of the cart, placed the young man upon it, took the black cap, and were just pulling it down over his face. The Spanish soldiers awaited the order to fire. But just then the American and English Consuls rode up. The English Consul sprang out of the carriage and took the union jack, the British flag, and wrapped it around the man, and the American Consul wrapped around him the star-spangled banner, and then turning to the Spanish officers they said: "Fire upon those flags, if you dare." They did not dare to fire upon the flags. There were two great governments behind those flags. That was the secret of it.

"He brought me to the banqueting house, and His banner over me was love. . . . His left hand is under my head and His right hand doth embrace me" (Song Sol. ii. 4, 6). Thank God we can come under the banner to-day if we will. Any poor sinner can come under that banner to-day. His banner of love is over us. Blessed Gospel; blessed, precious, news. Believe it to-day; receive it into your heart; and enter into a new life. Let the love of God be shed abroad in your heart by the Holy Ghost to-day: it will drive away darkness; it will drive away gloom; it will drive away sin; and peace and joy shall be yours.

CHAPTER II.

THE GATEWAY INTO THE KINGDOM.

"Except a man be born again he cannot enter the kingdom of God."
(John iii. 3.)

There is no portion of the Word of God, perhaps, with which we are more familiar than this passage. I suppose if I were to ask those in any audience if they believed that Jesus Christ taught the doctrine of the New Birth, nine tenths of them would say: "Yes, I believe He did."

Now if the words of this text are true they embody one of the most solemn questions that can come before us. We can afford to be deceived about many things rather than about this one thing. Christ makes it very plain. He says, "Except a man be born again, he cannot *see* the Kingdom of God"—much less inherit it. This doctrine of the New Birth is therefore the foundation of all our hopes for the world to come. It is really the A B C of the Christian religion. My experience has been this—that if a man is unsound on this doctrine he will be unsound on almost every other fundamental doctrine in the Bible. A true understanding of this subject will help a man to solve a thousand difficulties that he may meet with in the Word of God. Things that before seemed very dark and mysterious will become very plain.

The doctrine of the New Birth upsets all false religion—all false views about the Bible and about God. A friend of mine once told me that in one of his after-meetings, a man came to him with a long list of questions written out for him to answer. He said: "If you can answer these questions satisfactorily, I have made up my mind to be a Christian." "Do you not think," said my friend, "that you had better come to Christ first? Then you can look into these questions." The man thought that perhaps he had better do so. After he had received Christ, he looked again at his list of questions; but then it seemed to him as if they had all been answered. Nicodemus came with his troubled mind, and Christ said to him, "Ye must be born again." He was treated altogether differently from what he expected; but I venture to say that was the most blessed night in all his life. To be "born again" is the greatest blessing that will ever come to us in this world.

Notice how the Scripture puts it. "Except a man be born again," "born from above,"* "born of the Spirit." From amongst a number of other passages where we find this word "EXCEPT," I would just name three. "Except ye repent, ye shall all likewise perish." (Luke xiii. 3, 5.) "Except ye be converted, and become as little children, ye shall not enter into the kingdom of heaven." (Matt. xviii. 3.) "Except your righteousness shall exceed the righteousness of the Scribes and Pharisees, ye shall in no case enter into the kingdom of heaven." (Matt. v. 20.) They all really mean the same thing.

I am so thankful that our Lord spoke of the New Birth to this ruler of the Jews, this doctor of the law, rather than to the woman at the well of Samaria, or to Matthew the publican, or to Zaccheus. If He had reserved his teaching on this great matter for these three, or such as these, people would have said: "Oh yes, these publicans and harlots need to be converted: but I am an upright man; I do not need to be converted." I suppose Nicodemus was one of the best specimens of the people of Jerusalem: there was nothing on record against him.

---

*John iii. 3. *Marginal reading.*

I think it is scarcely necessary for me to prove that we need to be born again before we are meet for heaven. I venture to say that there is no candid man but would say he is not fit for the kingdom of God, until he is born of another Spirit. The Bible teaches us that man by nature is lost and guilty, and our experience confirms this. We know also that the best and holiest man, if he turn away from God, will very soon fall into sin.

Now, let me say what Regeneration is not. It is not going to church. Very often I see people, and ask them if they are Christians. "Yes, of course I am; at least, I think I am: I go to church every Sunday." Ah, but this is not Regeneration. Others say, "I am trying to do what is right—am I not a Christian? Is not that a new birth?" No. What has that to do with being born again? There is yet another class —those who have "turned over a new leaf," and think they are regenerated. No; forming a new resolution is not being born again.

Nor will being baptized do you any good. Yet you hear people say, "Why, I have been baptized; and I was born again when I was baptized." They believe that because they were baptized into the church, they were baptized into the Kingdom of God. I tell you that it is utterly impossible. You may be baptized into the church, and yet not be baptized into the Son of God. Baptism is all right in its place. God forbid that I should say anything against it. But if you put that in the place of Regeneration—in the place of the New Birth—it is a terrible mistake. You cannot be baptized into the Kingdom of God. "Except a man be BORN AGAIN, he cannot see the Kingdom of God." If any one reading this rests his hopes on anything else—on any other foundation—I pray that God may sweep it away.

Another class say, "I go to the Lord's Supper; I partake uniformly of the Sacrament." Blessed ordinance! Jesus hath said that as often as ye do it ye commemorate His death. Yet, that is not being "born again;" that is not passing from death unto life. Jesus says plainly—and so plainly that there need not be any mistake about it—"Except a man be born of the Spirit, he cannot enter into the Kingdom of God." What has a sacrament to do with that? What has going to church to do with being born again?

Another man comes up and says, "I say my prayers regularly." Still I say that is not being born of the Spirit. It is a very solemn question, then, that comes up before us; and oh! that every reader would ask himself earnestly and faithfully: "Have I been born again? Have I been born of the Spirit? Have I passed from death unto life?"

There is a class of men who say that special religious meetings are very good for a certain class of people. They would be very good if you could get the drunkard there, or get the gambler there, or get other vicious people there—that would do a great deal of good. But "we do not need to be converted." To whom did Christ utter these words of wisdom? To Nicodemus. Who was Nicodemus? Was he a drunkard, a gambler, or a thief? No! No doubt he was one of the very best men in Jerusalem. He was an honorable Councillor; he belonged to the Sanhedrim; he held a very high position; he was an orthodox man; he was one of the very soundest men. And yet what did Christ say to him? "Except a man be born again, he *cannot see* the kingdom of God."

But I can imagine some one saying, "What am I to do? I cannot create life. I certainly cannot save myself." You certainly cannot; and we do not claim that you can. We tell you it is utterly impossible to make a man better without

Christ; but that is what men are trying to do. They are trying to patch up this "old Adam" nature. THERE MUST BE A NEW CREATION. Regeneration is a new creation; and if it is a new creation it must be the work of God. In the first chapter of Genesis man does not appear. There is no one there but God. Man is not there to take part. When God created the earth He was alone. When Christ redeemed the world He was alone.

"That which is born of the flesh is flesh; and that which is born of the Spirit is spirit." (John iii. 6.) The Ethiopian cannot change his skin, and the leopard cannot change his spots. You might as well try to make yourselves pure and holy without the help of God. It would be just as easy for you to do that as for the black man to wash himself white. A man might just as well try to leap over the moon as to serve God in the flesh. Therefore, "that which is born of the flesh is flesh; and that which is born of the Spirit is spirit."

Now God tells us in this chapter how we are to get into His kingdom. We are not to work our way in—not but that salvation is worth working for. We admit all that. If there were rivers and mountains in the way, it would be well worth while to swim those rivers, and climb those mountains. There is no doubt that salvation is worth all that effort; but we do not obtain it by our works. It is "to him that worketh not, but believeth" (Rom. iv. 5). We work because we are saved; we do not work to be saved. We work from the cross; but not towards it. It is written, "Work out your own salvation with fear and trembling" (Phil. ii. 12). Why, you must have your salvation before you can work it out. Suppose I say to my little boy, "I want you to spend that hundred dollars carefully." "Well," he says, "let me have the hundred dollars; and I will be careful how I spend it." I remember when I first left home and went to Boston; I had spent all my money, and I went to the post-office three times a day. I knew there was only one mail a day from home; but I thought by some possibility there might be a letter for me. At last I received a letter from my little sister; and oh, how glad I was to get it. She had heard that there were a great many pick-pockets in Boston, and a large part of that letter was to urge me to be very careful not to let anybody pick my pocket. Now I required to have something in my pocket before I could have it picked. So you must have salvation before you can work it out.

When Christ cried out on Calvary, "It is finished!" He meant what He said. All that men have to do now is just to accept of the work of Jesus Christ. There is no hope for man or woman so long as they are trying to work out salvation for themselves. I can imagine there are some people who will say, as Nicodemus possibly did, "This is a very mysterious thing." I see the scowl on that Pharisee's brow as he says, "How can these things be?" It sounds very strange to his ear. "Born again; born of the Spirit! How can these things be?" A great many people say, "You must reason it out; but if you do not reason it out, do not ask us to believe it." I can imagine a great many people saying that. When you ask me to reason it out, I tell you frankly I cannot do it. "The wind bloweth where it listeth, and thou hearest the sound thereof, but canst not tell whence it cometh and whither it goeth: so is every one that is born of the Spirit." (John iii. 8.) I do not understand everything about the wind. You ask me to reason it out. I cannot. It may blow due north here, and a hundred miles away due south. I may go up a few hundred feet, and find it blowing in an entirely opposite direction from what it is down here. You ask me to explain these currents of wind; but suppose that, because I cannot explain them, and do not understand them, I were to take my stand and assert, "Oh, there is no such thing as wind." I can imagine some little girl saying, "I know more about it than that man does; often have I heard the wind, and felt it blowing against my face;" and she might say, "Did not the wind blow my umbrella out of my hands the other day? and did I not see it blow a man's hat off in the street? Have I not seen it blow the trees in the forest, and the growing corn in the country?"

You might just as well tell me that there is no such thing as wind, as tell me there is no such thing as a man being born of the Spirit. I have felt the spirit of God working in my heart, just as really and as truly as I have felt the wind blowing in my face. I cannot reason it out. There are a great many things I cannot reason out, but which I believe. I never could reason out the creation. I can see the world, but I cannot tell how God made it out of nothing. But almost every man will admit there was a creative power.

There are a great many things that I cannot explain and cannot reason out, and yet that I believe. I heard a commercial traveler say that he had heard that the ministry and religion of Jesus Christ were matters of revelation and not of investigation. "When it pleased God to reveal His Son in Me," says Paul (Gal. i, 15, 16). There was a party of young men together, going up the country; and on their journey they made up their minds not to believe anything they could not reason out. An old man heard them; and presently he said, "I heard you say you would not believe anything you could not reason out." "Yes," they said, "that is so." "Well," he said, "coming down on the train to-day, I noticed some geese, some sheep, some swine, and some cattle all eating grass. Can you tell me by what process that same grass was turned into hair, feathers, bristles and wool? Do you believe it is a fact?" "Oh yes," they said, "we cannot help believing that, though we fail to understand it." "Well," said the old man, "I cannot help believing in Jesus Christ." And I cannot help believing in the regeneration of man, when I see men who have been reclaimed, when I see men who have been reformed. Have not some of the very worst men been regenerated—been picked up out of the pit, and had their fect set upon the Rock, and a new song put in their mouths? Their tongues were cursing and blaspheming; and now are occupied in praising God. Old things have passed away, and all things have become new. They are not reformed only, but REGENERATED—new men in Christ Jesus.

Down there in the dark alleys of one of our great cities is a poor drunkard. I think if you want to get near hell, you should go to a poor drunkard's home. Go to the house of that poor miserable drunkard. Is there anything more like hell on earth? See the want and distress that reign there. But hark! A footstep is heard at the door, and the children run and hide themselves. The patient wife waits to meet the man. He has been her torment. Many a time she has borne about the marks of his blows for weeks. Many a time that strong right hand has been brought down on her defenseless head. And now she waits expecting to hear his oaths and suffer his brutal treatment. He comes in and says to her: "I have been to the meeting; and I heard there that if I will I can be converted. I believe that God is able to save me." Go down to that house again in a few weeks: and what a change! As you approach you hear some one singing. It is not the song of a reveller, but the strains of that good old hymn, "Rock of Ages." The children are no longer afraid of the man, but cluster around his knee. His wife is near him, her face lit up with a happy glow. Is not that a picture of Regeneration? I can take you to many such homes, made happy by the regenerating power of the religion of Christ.

What men want is the power to overcome temptation, the power to lead a right life.

The only way to get into the kingdom of God is to be "born" into it. The law of this country requires that the President should be born in the country. When foreigners come to our shores they have no right to complain against such a law, which forbids them from ever becoming Presidents. Now, has not God a right to make a law that all those who become heirs of eternal life must be "born" into His kingdom?

An unregenerated man would rather be in hell than in heaven. Take a man whose heart is full of corruption and wickedness, and place him in heaven among the pure, the holy and the redeemed; and he would not want to stay there. Certainly, if we are to be happy in heaven we must begin to make a heaven here on earth. Heaven is a prepared place for a prepared people. If a gambler or a blasphemer were taken out of the streets of New York and placed on the crystal pavement of heaven and under the shadow of the tree of life, he would say, "I do not want to stay here." If men were taken to heaven just as they are by nature, without having their hearts regenerated, there would be another rebellion in heaven. Heaven is filled with a company of those who have been TWICE BORN.

In the 14th and 15th verses of this chapter we read "As Moses lifted up the serpent in the wilderness, even so must the Son of Man be lifted up; that WHOSOEVER believeth in Him should not perish, but have eternal life." "**WHOSOEVER.**" Mark that! Let me tell you who are unsaved what God has done for you. He has done everything that He could do toward your salvation. You need not wait for God to do anything more. In one place he asks the question, what more could he have done (Isaiah v. 4). He sent His prophets, and they killed them; then He sent His beloved Son, and they murdered Him. Now He has sent the Holy Spirit to convince us of sin, and to show how we are to be saved.

In this chapter we are told how men are to be saved, namely, by Him who was lifted up on the cross. Just as Moses lifted up the brazen serpent in the wilderness, so must the Son of Man be lifted up, "that whosoever believeth in Him should not perish, but have eternal life." Some men complain and say that it is very unreasonable that they should be held responsible for the sin of a man six thousand years ago. It was not long ago that a man was talking to me about this injustice, as he called it. If a man thinks he is going to answer God in that way, I tell you it will not do him any good. If you are lost, it will not be on account of Adam's sin.

Let me illustrate this; and perhaps you will be better able to understand it. Suppose I am dying of consumption, which I inherited from my father or mother. I did not get the disease by any fault of my own, by any neglect of my health; I inherited it, let us suppose. A friend happens to come along: he looks at me, and says: "Moody, you are in a consumption." I reply, "I know it very well; I do not want any one to tell me that." "But," he says, "there is a remedy." "But, sir, I do not believe it. I have tried the leading physicians in this country and in Europe; and they tell me there is no hope." "But you know me, Moody; you have known me for years." "Yes, sir." "Do you think, then, I would tell you a falsehood?" "No." "Well, ten years ago I was as far gone. I was given up by the physicians to die; but I took this medicine and it cured me. I am perfectly well: look at me." I say that it is "a very strange case." "Yes, it may be strange; but it is a fact. This medicine cured me: take this medicine, and it will cure you. Although it has cost me a great deal, it shall not cost you anything. Do not make light of it, I beg of you." "Well," I say, "I should like to believe you; but this is contrary to my reason."

Hearing this, my friend goes away and returns with another friend, and that one testifies to the same thing. I am still disbelieving; so he goes away, and brings in another friend, and another, and another, and another; and they all testify to the same thing. They say they were as bad as myself; that they took the same medicine that has been offered to me; and that it has cured them. My friend then hands me the medicine. I dash it to the ground; I do not believe in its saving power; I die. The reason is then that I spurned the remedy. So, if you perish, it will not be because Adam fell; but because you spurned the remedy offered to save you. You will choose darkness rather than light. "How then shall ye escape, if ye neglect so great salvation?" There is no hope for you if you neglect the remedy. It does no good to look at the wound. If we had been in the Israelitish camp and had been bitten by one of the fiery serpents, it would have done us no good to look at the wound. Looking at the wound will never save any onè. What you must do is to look at the Remedy—look away to Him who hath power to save you from your sin.

Behold the camp of the Israelites; look at the scene that is pictured to your eyes! Many are dying because they neglect the remedy that is offered. In that arid desert is many a short and tiny grave; many a child has been bitten by the fiery serpents. Fathers and mothers are bearing away their children. Over yonder they are just burying a mother; a loved mother is about to be laid in the earth. All the family, weeping, gather around the beloved form. You hear the mournful cries; you see the bitter tears. The father is being borne away to his last resting place. There is wailing going up all over the camp. Tears are pouring down for thousands who have passed away; thousands more are dying; and the plague is raging from one end of the camp to the other.

I see in one tent an Israelitish mother bending over the form of a beloved boy just coming into the bloom of life, just budding into manhood. She is wiping away the sweat of death that is gathering upon his brow. Yet a little while, and his eyes are fixed and glassy, for life is ebbing fast away. The mother's heart-strings are torn and bleeding. All at once she hears a noise in the camp. A great shout goes up. What does it mean? She goes to the door of the tent. "What is the noise in the camp?" she asks those passing by. And some one says: "Why, my good woman, have you not heard the good news that has come into the camp?" "No," says the woman, "Good news! What is it?" "Why, have you not heard about it? God has provided a remedy." "What! for the bitten Israelities? Oh, tell me what the remedy is!" "Why, God has instructed Moses to make a brazen serpent, and to put it on a pole in the middle of the camp; and He has declared that whosoever looks upon it shall live. The shout that you hear is the shout of the people when they see the serpent lifted up." The mother goes back into the tent, and she says: "My boy, I have good news to tell you. You need not die! My boy, my boy, I have come with good tidings; you can live!" He is already getting stupefied; he is so weak he cannot walk to the door of the tent. She puts her strong arms under him and lifts him up. "Look yonder; look right there under the hill!" But the boy does not see anything; he says—"I do not see anything; what is it, mother?" And she says: "Keep looking, and you will see it." At last he catches a glimpse of the glistening serpent; and lo, he is well! And thus it is with many a young convert. Some men say, "Oh, we do not believe in sudden conversions." How long did it take to cure that boy? How long did it take to cure those serpent-bitten Israelites? It was just a look; and they were well.

That Hebrew boy is a young convert. I can fancy that I see him now calling on all those who were with him to praise God. He sees another young man bitten as he was; and he runs up to him and tells him, "You need not die." "Oh," the young man replies, "I cannot live; it is not possible. There is not a physician in Israel who can cure me." He does not know that he need not die. "Why, have you not heard the news? God has provided a remedy." "What remedy?" "Why, God has told Moses to lift up a brazen serpent, and has said that none of those who look upon that serpent shall die." I can just imagine the young man. He may be what you call an intellectual young man. He says to the young convert: "You do not think I am going to believe anything like that? If the physicians in Israel cannot cure me, how do you think that an old brass serpent on a pole is going to cure me?" "Why, sir, I was as bad as yourself!" "You do not say so!" "Yes, I do." "That is the most astonishing thing I ever heard," says the young man: "I wish you would explain the philosophy of it." "I cannot. I only know that I looked at that serpent, and I was cured: that did it. I just looked; that is all. My mother told me the reports that were being heard through the camp; and I just believed what my mother said, and I am perfectly well." "Well, I do not believe you were bitten as badly as I have been." The young man pulls up his sleeve. "Look there! That mark shows where I was bitten; and I tell you I was worse than you are." "Well, if I understood the philosophy of it I would look and get well." "Let your philosophy go: *look and live.*" "But, sir, you ask me to do an unreasonable thing. If God had said, Take the brass and rub it into the wound, there might be something in the brass that would cure the bite.

Young man, explain the philosophy of it." I have often seen people before me who have talked in that way. But the young man calls in another, and takes him into the tent, and says: "Just tell him how the Lord saved you;" and he tells just the same story; and he calls in others, and they all say the same thing.

The young man says it is a very strange thing. "If the Lord had told Moses to go and get some herbs, or roots, and stew them, and take the decoction as a medicine, there would be something in that. But it is so contrary to nature to do such a thing as look at the serpent, that I cannot do it." At length his mother, who has been out in the camp, comes in, and she says, "My boy, I have just the best news in the world for you. I was in the camp, and I saw hundreds who were very far gone, and they are all perfectly well now." The young man says: "I should like to get well; it is a very painful thought to die; I want to go into the promised land, and it is terrible to die here in this wilderness; but the fact is—I do not understand the remedy. It does not appeal to my reason. I cannot believe that I can get well in a moment." And the young man dies in consequence of his own unbelief.

God provided a remedy for this bitten Israelite—"Look and live!" And there is eternal life for every poor sinner. Look, and you can be saved, my reader, this very hour. God has provided a remedy; and it is offered to all. The trouble is, a great many people are looking at the pole. Do not look at the pole; that is the church. You need not look at the church; the church is all right, but the church cannot save you. Look beyond the pole. Look at the Crucified One. Look to Calvary. Bear in mind, sinner, that Jesus died for all. You need not look at ministers; they are just God's chosen instruments to hold up the Remedy, to hold up Christ.

And so, my friends, take your eyes off from men; take your eyes off from the church. Lift them up to Jesus; who took away the sin of the world, and there will be life for you from this hour.

Thank God, we do not require an education to teach us how to look. That little girl, that little boy, only four years old, who cannot read, can look. When the father is coming home, the mother says to her little boy, "Look! look! look!" and the little child learns to look long before he is a year old. And that is the way to be saved. It is to look at the Lamb of God "who taketh away the sin of the world;" and there is life this moment for every one who is willing to look.

Some men say, "I wish I knew how to be saved." Just take God at His word and trust His Son this very day—this very hour—this very moment. He will save you, if you will trust Him. I imagine I hear some one saying, "I do not feel the bite as much as I wish I did. I know I am a sinner, and all that; but I do not feel the bite enough." How much does God want you to feel it?

When I was in Belfast I knew a doctor who had a friend, a leading surgeon there; and he told me that the surgeon's custom was, before performing any operation, to say to the patient, "Take a good look at the wound, and then fix your eyes on me; and do not take them off till I get through." I thought at the time that was a good illustration. Sinner, take a good look at your wound; and then fix your eyes on Christ, and do not take them off. It is better to look at the Remedy than at the wound. See what a poor wretched sinner you are; and then look at the Lamb of God who "taketh away the sin of the world." He died for the ungodly and the sinner. Say "I will take Him!" And may God help you to lift your eye to the Man on Calvary. And as the

Israelites looked upon the serpent and were healed, so may you look and live.

After the battle of Pittsburgh Landing I was in a hospital at Murfreesbro.' In the middle of the night I was aroused and told that a man in one of the wards wanted to see me. I went to him and he called me "chaplain"—I was not the chaplain—and said he wanted me to help him die. And I said, "I would take you right up in my arms and carry you into the kingdom of God if I could; but I cannot do it: I cannot help you die!" And he said, "Who can?" I said, "The Lord Jesus Christ can—He came for that purpose." He shook his head, and said, "He cannot save me; I have sinned all my life." And I said, "But He came to save sinners." I thought of his mother in the north, and I was sure that she was anxious that he should die in peace; so I resolved I would stay with him. I prayed two or three times, and repeated all the promises I could; for it was evident that in a few hours he would be gone. I said I wanted to read him a conversation that Christ had with a man who was anxious about his soul. I turned to the third chapter of John. His eyes were riveted on me; and when I came to the 14th and 15th verses—the passage before us—he caught up the words, "As Moses lifted up the serpent in the wilderness, even so must the Son of Man be lifted up; that whosoever believeth in Him should not perish, but have eternal life." He stopped me and said, "Is that there?" I said "Yes." He asked me to read it again; and I did so. He leant his elbows on the cot and clasping his hands together, said, "That's good; won't you read it again?" I read it the third time; and then went on with the rest of the chapter. When I had finished, his eyes were closed, his hands were folded, and there was a smile on his face. Oh, how it was lit up! What a change had come over it! I saw his lips quivering, and leaning over him I heard in a faint whisper, "As Moses lifted up the serpent in the wilderness, even so must the Son of Man be lifted up; that whosoever believeth in Him should not perish, but have eternal life." He opened his eyes and said, "That's enough; don't read any more." He lingered a few hours, pillowing his head on those two verses; and then went up in one of Christ's chariots, to take his seat in the kingdom of God.

Christ said to Nicodemus: "Except a man be born again, he cannot see the kingdom of God." You may see many countries; but there is one country—the land of Beulah, which John Bunyan saw in vision—you shall never behold, unless you are born again—regenerated by Christ. You can look abroad and see many beautiful trees; but the tree of life, you shall never behold, unless your eyes are made clear by faith in the Saviour. You may see the beautiful rivers of the earth—you may ride upon their bosoms; but bear in mind that your eye will never rest upon the river which bursts out from the Throne of God and flows through the upper Kingdom, unless you are born again. God has said it; and not man. You will never see the kingdom of God except you are born again. You may see the kings and lords of the earth; but the King of kings and Lord of lords you will never see except you are born again. When you are in London you may go to the Tower and see the crown of England, which is worth thousands of dollars, and is guarded there by soldiers; but bear in mind that your eye will never rest upon the crown of life except you are born again.

You may hear the songs of Zion which are sung here; but one song—that of Moses and the Lamb—the uncircumcised ear shall never hear; its melody will only gladden the ear of those who have been born again. You may look upon the beautiful mansions of earth, but bear in mind the mansions which Christ has gone to prepare you shall never see unless you are born again. It is God who says it. You may see ten thousand beautiful things in this world; but the city that Abraham caught a glimpse of—and from that time became a pilgrim and sojourner—you shall never see unless you are born again (Heb. xi. 8, 10—16). You may often be invited to marriage feasts here; but you will never attend the marriage supper of the Lamb except you are born again. It is God who says it, dear friend. You may be looking on the face of your sainted mother to-night, and feel that she is praying for you; but the time will come when you shall never see her more unless you are born again.

The reader may be a young man or a young lady who has recently stood by the bedside of a dying mother; and she may have said, "Be sure and meet me in heaven," and you made the promise. Ah! you shall never see her more, except you are born again. I believe Jesus of Nazareth, sooner than those infidels who say you do not need to be born again. Parents, if you hope to see your children who have gone before, you must be born of the Spirit. Possibly you are a father or a mother who has recently borne a loved one to the grave; and how dark your home seems! Never more will you see your child, unless you are born again. If you wish to be re-united to your loved one, you must be born again. I may be addressing a father or a mother who has a loved one up yonder. If you could hear that loved one's voice, it would say, "Come this way." Have you a sainted friend up yonder? Young man or young lady, have you not a mother in the world of light? If you could hear her speak, would not she say, "Come this way, my son,"—"Come this way, my daughter?" If you would ever see her more you must be born again.

We all have an Elder Brother there. Nearly nineteen hundred years ago He crossed over, and from the heavenly shores He is calling you to heaven. Let us turn our backs upon the world. Let us give a deaf ear to the world. Let us look to Jesus on the Cross and be saved. Then we shall one day see the King in His beauty, and we shall go no more out.

CHAPTER III.

THE TWO CLASSES.

"Two men went up into the temple to pray."—Luke xvii. 10.

I now want to speak of two classes: First, those who do not feel their need of a Saviour who have not been convinced of sin by the Spirit; and Second, those who are convinced of sin and cry, "What must I do to be saved?"

All inquirers can be ranged under two heads: they have either the spirit of the Pharisee, or the spirit of the publican. If a man having the spirit of the Pharisee comes into an after-meeting, I know of no better portion of Scripture to meet his case than Romans iii. 10: "As it is written, There is none righteous, no, not one: there is none that understandeth; there is none that seeketh after God." Paul is here speaking of the natural man. "They are all gone out of the way, they are together become unprofitable; there is none that doeth good, no, not one." And in the 17th verse and those which follow, we have "And the way of peace have they not known; there is no fear of God before their eyes. Now we know what things soever the law saith, it saith to them who are under the law; that every mouth may be stopped, and all the world may become guilty before God."

Then observe the last clause of verse 22: "For there is no difference; for all have sinned, and come short of the glory of God." Not part of the human family—but *all*—"have sinned, and come short of the glory of God." Another verse which has been very much used to convict men of their sin is

1 John i. 8: "If we say that we have no sin, we deceive ourselves, and the truth is not in us."

I remember that on one occasion we were holding meetings in an eastern city of forty thousand inhabitants; and a lady came and asked us to pray for her husband, whom she purposed bringing into the after meeting. I have traveled a good deal and met many pharisaical men; but this man was so clad in self-righteousness that you could not get the point of the needle of conviction in anywhere. I said to his wife: "I am glad to see your faith; but we cannot get near him; he is the most self-righteous man I ever saw." She said: "You *must!* My heart will break if these meetings end without his conversion." She persisted in bringing him; and I got almost tired of the sight of him.

But towards the close of our meetings of thirty days, he came up to me and put his trembling hand on my shoulder. The place in which the meetings were held was rather cold, and there was an adjoining room in which only the gas had been lighted; and he said to me, "Can't you come in here for a few minutes?" I thought that he was shaking from cold, and I did not particularly wish to go where it was colder. But he said: "I am the worst man in the State of Vermont. I want you to pray for me." I thought he had committed a murder, or some other awful crime; and I asked: "Is there any one sin that particularly troubles you?" And he said: "My whole life has been a sin. I have been a conceited, self-righteous Pharisee. I want you to pray for me." He was under deep conviction. Man could not have produced this result; but the Spirit had. About two o'clock in the morning light broke in upon his soul: and he went up and down the business street of the city and told what God had done for him; and has been a most active Christian ever since.

There are four other passages in dealing with inquirers, which were used by Christ Himself. "Verily, verily, I say unto thee, Except a man be born again, he cannot see the kingdom of God." (John iii. 3.)

In Luke xiii. 3, we read: "Except ye repent, ye shall all likewise perish."

In Matthew xviii., when the disciples came to Jesus to know who was to be the greatest in the kingdom of heaven, we are told that He took a little child and set him in the midst and said, "Verily I say unto you, Except ye be converted, and become as little children, ye shall not enter the kingdom of heaven" (xviii. 1-3).

There is another important "Except" in Matthew v. 20: "Except your righteousness shall exceed the righteousness of the Scribes and Pharisees, ye shall in no case enter the kingdom of heaven."

A man must be made meet before he will want to go into the kingdom of God. I would rather go into the kingdom with the younger brother than stay outside with the elder. Heaven would be hell to such an one. An elder brother who could not rejoice at his younger brother's return would not be "fit" for the kingdom of God. It is a solemn thing to contemplate; but the curtain drops and leaves him outside, and the younger brother within. To him the language of the Saviour under other circumstances seems appropriate: "Verily I say unto you, That the publicans and the harlots go into the kingdom of God before you" (Matt. xxi. 31).

A lady once came to me and wanted a favor for her daughter. She said: "You must remember I do not sympathize with you in your doctrine." I asked: "What is your trouble?" She said: "I think your abuse of the elder brother is horrible. I think he is a noble character." I said that I was willing to hear her defend him; but that it was a solemn thing to take up such a position; and that the elder brother needed to be converted as much as the younger. When people talk of being moral it is well to get them to take a good look at the old man pleading with his boy who would not go in.

But we will pass on now to the other class with which we have to deal. It is composed of those who are convinced of sin and from whom the cry comes as from the Philippian jailer, "What must I do to be saved?" To those who utter this penitential cry there is no necessity to administer the law. It is well to bring them straight to the Scripture: "Believe on the Lord Jesus Christ, and thou shalt be saved." (Acts xvi. 31). Many will meet you with a scowl and say, "I don't know what it is to believe; and though it is the law of heaven that they must believe, in order to be saved—yet they ask for something besides that. We are to tell them what, and where, and how, to believe.

In John iii. 35 and 36 we read: "The Father loveth the Son, and hath given all things into His hand. He that believeth on the Son HATH everlasting life; and he that believeth not the Son shall not see life; but the wrath of God abideth on him."

Now this looks reasonable. Man lost life by unbelief—by not believing God's word; and we got life back again by believing—by taking God at His word. In other words we get up where Adam fell down. He stumbled and fell over the stone of unbelief; and we are lifted up and stand upright by believing. When people say they cannot believe, show them chapter and verse, and hold them right to this one thing: "Has God ever broken His promise for these six thousand years?" The devil and men have been trying all the time and have not succeeded in showing that He has broken a single promise; and there would be a jubilee in hell to-day if one word that He has spoken could be broken. If a man says that he cannot believe it is well to press him on that one thing.

I can believe God better to-day than I can my own heart. "The heart is deceitful above all things, and desperately wicked: who can know it?" (Jer. xvii. 9). I can believe God better than I can myself. If you want to know the way of Life, believe that Jesus Christ is a personal Saviour; cut away from all doctrines and creeds, and come right to the heart of the Son of God. If you have been feeding on dry doctrine there is not much growth on that kind of food. Doctrines are to the soul what the streets which lead to the house of a friend who has invited me to dinner are to the body. They will lead me there if I take the right one; but if I remain in the streets my hunger will never be satisfied. Feeding on doctrines is like trying to live on dry husks; and lean indeed must the soul remain which partakes not of the Bread sent down from heaven.

Some ask: "How am I to get my heart warmed?" It is by believing. You do not get power to love and serve God until you believe.

The apostle John says: "If we receive the witness of men, the witness of God is greater: for this is the witness of God which He hath testified of His Son. He that believeth on the Son of God hath the witness in himself: he that believeth not God hath made Him a liar; because he believeth not the record that God gave of His Son. And this is the record, that God hath given to us eternal life, and this life is in His Son. He that hath the Son hath life; and he that hath not the Son of God hath not life" (1 John v. 9).

Human affairs would come to a standstill if we did not take the testimony of men. How should we get on in the ordinary intercourse of life, and how would commerce get on, if we disregarded men's testimony? Things social and commercial would come to a dead-lock within forty-eight hours! This is the drift of the apostle's argument here. "If we receive the witness of men, the witness of God is greater." God has borne witness to Jesus Christ. And if man can believe his fellow men who are frequently telling untruths and whom we are constantly finding unfaithful, why should we not take God at His word and believe His testimony?

Faith is a belief in testimony. It is not a leap in the dark, as some tell us. That would be no faith at all. God does not ask any man to believe without giving him something to believe. You might as well ask a man to see without eyes; to hear without ears; and to walk without feet—as to bid him believe without giving him something to believe.

When I started for California I procured a guide-book. This told me, that after leaving the State of Illinois, I should cross the Mississippi, and then the Missouri; get into Nebraska; then over the Rocky Mountains to the Mormon settlement at Salt Lake City, and by the way of the Sierra Nevada into San Francisco. I found the guide book all right as I went along; and I should have been a miserable sceptic if, having proved it to be correct three-fourths of the way, I had said that I would not believe it for the remainder of the journey.

Suppose a man, in directing me to the Post Office, gives me ten landmarks; and that, in my progress there, I find nine of them to be as he told me; I should have good reason to believe that I was coming to the Post Office.

And if, by believing, I get a new life, and a hope, a peace, a joy, and a rest to my soul, that I never had before; if I get self-control, and find that I have a power to resist evil and to do good, I have pretty good proof that I am in the right road to the "city which hath foundations, whose builder and maker is God." And if things have taken place, and are now taking place, as recorded in God's Word, I have good reason to conclude that what yet remains will be fulfilled. And yet people talk of doubting. There can be no true faith where there is fear. Faith is to take God at His word, unconditionally. There cannot be true peace where there is fear. "Perfect love casteth out fear." How wretched a wife would be if she doubted her husband! and how miserable a mother would feel if after her boy had gone away from home she had reason, from his neglect, to question that son's devotion! True love never has a doubt.

There are three things indispensable to faith—knowledge, assent, and appropriation.

We must know God. "And this is life eternal, that they might *know* Thee, the only true God, and Jesus Christ whom Thou hast sent" (John xvii. 3). Then we must not only give our assent to what we know; but we must lay hold of the truth. If a man simply give his assent to the plan of salvation, it will not save him: he must accept Christ as his Saviour. He must receive and appropriate Him.

Some say they cannot tell how a man's life can be affected by his belief. But let some one cry out that some building in which we happen to be sitting, is on fire; and see how soon we should act on our belief and get out. We are all the time influenced by what we believe. We cannot help it. And let a man believe the record that God has given of Christ, and it will very quickly affect his whole life.

Take John v. 24. There is enough truth in that one verse for every soul to rest upon for salvation. It does not admit the shadow of a doubt. "Verily, verily"—which means truly, truly—"I say unto you, He that heareth My word, and believeth on Him that sent Me, hath—*hath*—everlasting life, and shall not come into condemnation; but is passed from death unto life."

Now if a person really hears the word of Jesus and believes with the heart on God who sent the Son to be the Saviour of the world, and lays hold of and appropriates this great salvation, there is no fear of judgment. He will not be looking forward with dread to the Great White Throne; for we read in 1 John iv. 17: "Herein is our love made perfect, that we may have boldness in the day of judgment: because as He is, so are we in this world."

If we believe, there is for us no condemnation, no judgment. That is behind us, and passed; and we shall have boldness in the day of judgment.

I remember reading of a man who was on trial for his life. He had friends with influence; and they procured a pardon for him from the king on condition that he was to go through the trial, and be condemned. He went into court with the pardon in his pocket. The feeling ran very high against him, and the judge said that the court was shocked that he was so much unconcerned. But, when the sentence was pronounced, he pulled out the pardon, presented it, and walked out a free man. He has been pardoned; and so have we. Then let death come, we have nought to fear. All the grave-diggers in the world cannot dig a grave large enough and deep enough to hold eternal life; all the coffin-makers in the world cannot make a coffin large enough and tight enough to hold eternal life. Death has had his hand on Christ once, but never again.

Jesus said: "I am the Resurrection, and the Life: he that believeth in Me, though he were dead, yet shall he live: and whosoever liveth and believeth in Me shall never die" (John xi. 25, 26). And in the Apocalypse we read that the risen Saviour said to John, "I am He that liveth, and was dead; and, behold, I am alive for evermore" (Rev i. 18). Death cannot touch Him again.

We get life by believing. In fact we get more than Adam lost; for the redeemed child of God is heir to a richer and more glorious inheritance than Adam in Paradise could ever have conceived; yea, and that inheritance endures forever—it is inalienable.

I would much rather have my life hid with Christ in God than have lived in Paradise; for Adam might have sinned and fallen after being there ten thousand years. But the believer is safer, if these things become real to him. Let us make them a fact, and not a fiction. God has said it; and that is enough. Let us trust Him even where we cannot trace Him. Let the same confidence animate us that was in little Maggie as related in the following simple but touching incident which I read in the *Bible Treasury*:—

"I had been absent from home for some days, and was wondering, as I again draw near the homestead, if my little Maggie, just able to sit alone, would remember me. To test her memory, I stationed myself where I could see her, but could not be seen by her, and called her name in the familiar tone, 'Maggie!' She dropped her playthings, glanced around the room, and then looked down upon her toys. Again I repeated her name, 'Maggie!' when she once more surveyed the room; but, not seeing her *father's* face, she looked very sad, and slowly resumed her employment. Once more I called, 'Maggie!' when, dropping her playthings, and bursting into tears, she stretched out her arms in the direction whence the sound proceeded, knowing that, though she could not see him, her father *must be there*, FOR SHE KNEW HIS VOICE."

Now, we have power to see and to hear, and we have power to believe. It is all folly for the inquirers to take the ground that they cannot believe. They can, if they will. But the trouble with most people is that they have connected FEELING with BELIEVING. Now Feeling has nothing whatever to do with Believing. The Bible does not say—He that feeleth, or he that feeleth and believeth, hath everlasting life. Nothing of the kind. I cannot control my feelings. If I could, I should never feel ill, or have a headache or toothache. I I should be well all the while. But I can believe God; and if we get our feet on that rock, let doubts and fears come and the waves surge around us, the anchor will hold.

Some people are all the time looking at their faith. Faith is the hand that takes the blessing. I heard this illustration of a beggar. Suppose you were to meet a man in the street whom you had known for years as being accustomed to beg; and you offered him some money, and he were to say to you: "I thank you; I don't want your money: I am not a beggar." "How is that?" "Last night a man put a thousand dollars into my hands." "He did! How did you know it was good money?" "I took it to the bank and deposited it and have got a bank book." "How did you get this gift?" "I asked for alms; and after the gentleman talked with me he took out a thousand dollars in money and put it in my hand." "How do you know that he put it in the right hand?" "What do I care about which hand; so that I have got the money." Many people are always thinking whether the faith by which they lay hold of Christ is the right kind—but what is far more essential is to see that we have the right kind of Christ.

Faith is the eye of the soul; and who would ever think of taking out an eye to see if it were the right kind so long as the sight was perfect? It is not my taste, but it is what I taste, that satisfies my appetite. So, dear friends, it is taking God at His Word that is the means of our salvation. The truth cannot be made too simple.

There is a man living in the city of New York who has a home on the Hudson River. His daughter and her family went to spend the winter with him; and in the course of the season the scarlet fever broke out. One little girl was put in quarantine, to be kept separate from the rest. Every morning the old grandfather used to go and bid his grandchild, "Good-bye," before going to his business. On one of these occasions the little thing took the old man by the hand, and, leading him to a corner of the room, without saying a word she pointed to the floor where she had arranged some small crackers so they would spell out, "Grandpa, I want a box of paints." He said nothing. On his return home he hung up his overcoat and went to the room as usual: when his little grandchild, without looking to see if her wish had been complied with, took him into the same corner, where he saw spelled out in the same way, "Grandpa, I thank you for the box of paints." The old man would not have missed gratifying the child for anything. That was faith.

Faith is taking God at His Word; and those people who want some token are always getting into trouble. We want to come to this: GOD SAYS IT—LET US BELIEVE IT.

But some say, Faith is the gift of God. So is the air; but you have to breathe it. So is bread; but you have to eat it. So is water; but you have to drink it. Some are wanting a miraculous kind of feeling. That is not faith. "Faith cometh by hearing, and hearing by the Word of God" (Rom. x. 17). That is whence faith comes. It is not for me to sit down and wait for faith to come stealing over me with a strange sensation; but it is for me to take God at His Word. And you cannot believe, unless you have something to believe. So take the Word as it is written, and appropriate it, and lay hold of it.

In John vi. 47, 48 we read: "Verily, verily, I say unto you, He that believeth on Me hath everlasting life. I am that Bread of life." There is the bread right at hand. Partake of it. I might have thousands of loaves within my home, and as many hungry men in waiting. They might assent to the fact that the bread was there; but unless they each took a loaf and commenced eating, their hunger would not be satisfied. So Christ is the Bread of heaven; and as the body feeds on natural food, so the soul must feed on Christ.

If a drowning man sees a rope thrown out to rescue him he must lay hold of it; and in order to do so he must let go everything else. If a man is sick he must take the medicine —for simply looking at it will not cure him. A knowledge of Christ will not help the inquirer, unless he believes in Him, and takes hold of Him, as his only hope. The bitten Israelites might have believed that the serpent was lifted up; but unless they had looked they would not have lived (Num. xxi. 6–9).

I believe that a certain line of steamers will convey me across the ocean, because I have tried it: but this will not help another man who may want to go, unless he acts upon my knowledge. So a knowledge of Christ does not help us unless we act upon it. That is what it is to believe on the Lord Jesus Christ. It is to act on what we believe. As a man steps on board a steamer to cross the Atlantic, so we must take Christ and make a commitment of our souls to Him; and He has promised to keep all who put their trust in Him. To believe on the Lord Jesus Christ, is simply to take Him at His word.

CHAPTER IV.

WORDS OF COUNSEL.

"A bruised reed shall He not break."—ISAIAH xlii. 3; MATT. xii. 20.

IT is dangerous for those who are seeking salvation to lean upon the experience of other people. Many are waiting for a repetition of the experience of their grandfather or grandmother. I had a friend who was converted in a field; and he thinks the whole town ought to go down into that meadow and be converted. Another was converted under a bridge; and he thinks that if any enquirer were to go there he would find the Lord. The best thing for the anxious is to go right to the Word of God. If there are any persons in the world to whom the Word ought to be very precious it is those who are asking how to be saved.

For instance a man may say, "I have no strength." Let him turn to Romans v. 6. "For when we were yet without strength, in due time Christ died for the ungodly." It is because we have no strength that we need Christ. He has come to give strength to the weak.

Another may say, "I cannot see." Christ says, "I am the Light of the world" (John viii. 12). He came, not only to give light, but "to open the blind eyes" (Isa. xlii. 7).

Another may say, "I do not think a man can be saved all at once." A person holding that view was in the Enquiry-room one night; and I drew his attention to Romans vi. 23. "The wages of sin is death; but the *gift* of God is eternal life, through Jesus Christ our Lord." How long does it take to accept a gift? There must be a moment when you have it not, and another when you have it—a moment when it is another's, and the next when it is yours. It does not take six months to get eternal life. It may however in some cases be like the mustard seed, very small at the commencement. Some people are converted so gradually that, like the morning light, it is impossible to tell when the dawn began; while, with others, it is like the flashing of a meteor, and the truth bursts upon them suddenly.

I would not go across the street to prove when I was converted; but what is important is for me to know that I really have been.

It may be that a child has been so carefully trained that it is impossible to tell when the new birth began; but there must have been a moment when the change took place, and when he became a partaker of the Divine nature.

Some people do not believe in SUDDEN CONVERSION. But I will challenge any one to show a conversion in the New Testament that was not instantaneous. "As Jesus passed by He saw Levi, the son of Alpheus, sitting at the receipt of custom, and said unto him, 'Follow Me': and he arose and followed Him" (Matt. ix. 9). Nothing could be more sudden than that.

Zaccheus, the publican, sought to see Jesus; and because he was little of stature he climbed up a tree. When Jesus came to the place He looked up and saw him, and said, "Zaccheus, make haste, and come down" (Luke xix. 5). His conversion must have taken place somewhere between the branch and the ground. We are told that he received Jesus joyfully, and said, "Behold, Lord, the half of my goods I give to the poor; and if I have taken anything from any man by false accusation, I restore him fourfold" (Luke xix. 8). Very few in these days could say that in proof of their conversion.

The whole house of Cornelius was converted suddenly; for as Peter preached Christ to him and his company the Holy Ghost fell on them, and they were baptized. (Acts x.)

On the day of Pentecost three thousand gladly received the Word. They were not only converted, but they were baptized the same day. (Acts ii.)

And when Philip talked to the eunuch, as they went on their way, the eunuch said to Philip, "See, here is water: what doth hinder me to be baptized?" Nothing hindered. And Philip said, "If thou believest with all thine heart, thou mayest." And they both went down into the water; and the man of great authority under Candace, the queen of the Ethiopians, was baptized, and went on his way rejoicing. (Acts viii. 26—38.) You will find all through Scripture that conversions were sudden and instantaneous.

A man has been in the habit of stealing money from his employer. Suppose he has taken $1,000 in twelve months; should we tell him to take $500 the next year, and less the next year, and the next, until in five years the sum taken would be only $50? That would be upon the same principle as gradual conversion.

If such a person were brought before the court and pardoned, because he could not change his mode of life all at once, it would be considered a very strange proceeding.

But the Bible says, "Let him that stole steal no more" (Eph. iv. 28). It is "right about face!" Suppose a person is in the habit of cursing one hundred times a day: should we advise him not to utter more than ninety oaths the following day, and eighty the next day; so that in the course of time he would get rid of the habit? The Saviour says, "Swear not at all." (Matt. v. 34.)

Suppose another man is in the habit of getting drunk and beating his wife twice a month; if he only did so once a month, and then only once in six months, that would be, upon the same ground, as reasonable as gradual conversion. Suppose Ananias had been sent to Paul, when he was on his way to Damascus breathing out threatenings and slaughter against the disciples, and casting them into prison, to tell him not to kill so many as he intended; and to let enmity die out of his heart gradually, but not all at once. Suppose he had been told that it would not do to stop breathing out threatenings and slaughter, and to commence preaching Christ all at once, because the philosophers would say that the change was so sudden it would not hold out; this would be the same kind of reasoning as is used by those who do not believe in instantaneous conversion.

Then another class say that they are afraid that they will not hold out. This is a numerous and very hopeful class. I like to see a man distrust himself. It is a good thing to get such to look to God, and to remember that it is not he who holds God, but that it is God who holds him. Some want to get hold of Christ; but the thing is to get Christ to take hold of you in answer to prayer. Let such read Psalm cxxi.; "I will lift up mine eyes unto the hills, from whence cometh my help. My help cometh from the Lord, which made heaven and earth. He will not suffer thy foot to be moved: He that keepeth thee will not slumber. Behold, He that keepeth Israel shall neither slumber nor sleep. The Lord is thy keeper; the Lord is thy shade upon thy right hand. The sun shall not smite thee by day, nor the moon by night. The Lord shall preserve thee from all evil: He shall preserve thy soul. The Lord shall preserve thy going out and thy coming in, from this time forth, and even for evermore."

Some one calls that the traveler's psalm. It is a beautiful psalm for those of us who are pilgrims through this world; and one with which we should be well acquainted.

God can do what He has done before. He kept Joseph in Egypt; Moses before Pharaoh; Daniel in Babylon; and enabled Elijah to stand before Ahab in that dark day. And I am so thankful that these I have mentioned were men of like passions with ourselves. It was God who made them so great. What man wants is to look to God. Real true faith is man's weakness leaning on God's strength. When man has no strength, if he leans on God he becomes powerful. The trouble is that we have too much strength and confidence in ourselves.

Again in Hebrews vi. 17, 18: "Wherein God, willing more abundantly to show unto the heirs of promise the immutability of His counsel, confirmed it by an oath that by two immutable things, in which it was impossible for God to lie, we might have a strong consolation, who have fled for refuge to lay hold upon the hope set before us: which hope we have as an anchor of the soul, both sure and steadfast, and which entereth into that within the vail; whither the Forerunner is for us entered, even Jesus, made an high priest for ever after the order of Melchisedec."

Now these are precious verses to those who are afraid of falling, who fear that they will not hold out. It is God's work to hold. It is the Shepherd's business to keep the sheep. Who ever heard of the sheep going to bring back the shepherd? People have an idea that they have to keep themselves and Christ too. It is a false idea. It is the work of the Shepherd to look after them, and to take care of those who trust Him. And He has promised to do it. I once heard that when a sea captain was dying he said, "Glory to God; the anchor holds." He trusted in Christ. His anchor had taken hold of the solid rock. An Irishman said, on one occasion, that "he trembled; but the Rock never did." We want to get sure footing.

In 2 Timothy i. 12 Paul says: "I know whom I have believed, and am persuaded that He is able to keep that which I have committed unto Him against that day." That was Paul's persuasion.

During the late war of the rebellion, one of the chaplains, going through the hospitals, came to a man who was dying. Finding that he was a Christian, he asked to what persuasion he belonged, and was told "Paul's persuasion." "Is he a Methodist?" he asked; for the Methodists all claim Paul. "No." "Is he a Presbyterian?" for the Presbyterians lay special claim to Paul. "No," was the answer. "Does he belong to the Episcopal Church?" for all the Episcopalian brethren contend that they have a claim to the Chief Apostle. "No," he was not an Episcopalian. "Then, to what persuasion does he belong?" "I am persuaded that He is able to keep that which I have committed unto Him against that day." It is a grand persuasion; and it gave the dying soldier rest in a dying hour.

Let those who fear that they will not hold out turn to the 24th verse of the Epistle of Jude: "Now unto Him that is able to keep you from falling, and to present you faultless before the presence of His glory with exceeding joy."

Then look at Isaiah xli. 10: "Fear thou not; for I am with thee: be not dismayed; for I am thy God: I will strengthen thee; yea, I will help thee; yea, I will uphold thee with the right hand of My righteousness."

Then see verse 13: "For I the Lord thy God will hold thy right hand, saying unto thee, Fear not; I will help thee."

Now if God has got hold of my right hand in His, cannot He hold me and keep me? Has not God the power to keep? The great God who made heaven and earth can keep a poor sinner like you and like me if we trust Him. To refrain from feeling confidence in God for fear of falling—would be like a man who refused a pardon, for fear that he should get into prison again; or a drowning man who refused to be rescued, for fear of falling into the water again.

Many men look forth at the Christian life, and fear that they will not have sufficient strength to hold out to the end. They forget the promise that "as thy days, thy strength" (Deut. xxxiii. 25). It reminds me of the pendulum to the clock which grew disheartened at the thought of having to travel so many thousands of miles; but when it reflected that the distance was to be accomplished by "tick, tick, tick," it took fresh courage to go its daily journey. So it is the special privilege of the Christian to commit himself to the keeping of his heavenly Father and to trust Him day by day. It is a comforting thing to know that the Lord will not begin the good work without also finishing it.

There are two kinds of sceptics—one class with honest difficulties; and another class who delight only in discussion. I used to think that this latter class would always be a thorn in my flesh; but they do not prick me now. I expect to find them right along the journey. Men of this stamp used to hang around Christ to entangle Him in His talk. They come into our meetings to hold a discussion. To all such I would commend Paul's advice to Timothy: "But foolish and unlearned questions avoid; knowing that they do gender strifes." (2 Tim. ii. 23.) Unlearned questions! Many young converts make a woful mistake. They think they are to defend the whole Bible. I knew very little of the Bible when I was first converted; and I thought that I had to defend it from beginning to end against all comers; but a Boston infidel got hold of me, floored all my arguments at once, and discouraged me. But I have got over that now. There are many things in the Word of God that I do not profess to understand.

When I am asked what I do with them, I say, "I don't do anything."

"How do you explain them?" "I don't explain them."

"What do you do with them?" "Why, I believe them."

And when I am told, "I would not believe anything that I do not understand," I simply reply that I do.

There are many things which were dark and mysterious five years ago, on which I have since had a flood of light; and I expect to be finding out something fresh about God throughout eternity. I make a point of not discussing disputed passages of Scripture. An old divine has said that some people, if they want to eat fish, commence by picking the bones. I leave such things till I have light on them. I am not bound to explain what I do not comprehend. "The secret things belong unto the Lord our God: but those things which are revealed belong unto us, and to our children, for ever" (Deut. xxix. 29); and these I take, and eat, and feed upon, in order to get spiritual strength.

Then there is a little sound advice in Titus iii. 9. "But avoid foolish questions, and genealogies, and contentions, and strivings about the law; for they are unprofitable and vain."

But now here comes an honest sceptic. With him I would deal as tenderly as a mother with her sick child. I have no sympathy with those people who, because a man is sceptical, cast him off and will have nothing to do with him.

I was in an Inquiry-meeting, some time ago, and I handed over to a Christian lady, whom I had known some time, one who was sceptical. On looking round soon after I noticed the enquirer marching out of the hall. I asked, "Why have you let her go?" "Oh, she is a sceptic!" was the reply. I ran to the door and got her to stop, and introduced her to another Christian worker who spent over an hour in conversation and prayer with her. He visited her and her husband; and, in the course of a week, that intelligent lady cast off her scepticism and came out an active Christian. It took time, tact, and prayer; but if a person of this class is honest we ought to deal with such an one as the Master would have us.

Here are a few passages for doubting enquirers:

"If any man will do His will, he shall know of the doctrine, whether it be of God, or whether I speak of myself" (John vii. 17). If a man is not willing to do the will of God he will not know the doctrine. There is no class of sceptics who are ignorant of the fact that God desires them to give up sin; and if a man is willing to turn from sin and take the light and thank Him for what He does give, and not expect to have light on the whole Bible all at once, he will get more light day by day; make progress step by step; and be led right out of darkness into the clear light of heaven.

In Daniel xii. 10 we are told: "Many shall be purified, and made white, and tried: but the wicked shall do wickedly; and none of the wicked shall understand; but the wise shall understand."

Now God will never reveal His secrets to His enemies. Never! And if a man persists in living in sin he will not know the doctrines of God.

"The secret of the Lord is with them that fear Him; and He will show them His covenant" (Ps. xxv. 14).

And in John xv. 15 we read: "Henceforth I call you not servants; for the servant knoweth not what his Lord doeth: but I have called you friends; for all things that I have heard of my Father I have made known unto you." When you become friends of Christ you will know His secrets. The Lord said, "Shall I hide from Abraham the things which I do?" (Gen. xviii. 17).

Now those who resemble God are the most likely to understand God. If a man is not willing to turn from sin he will not know God's will, nor will God reveal His secrets to him. But if a man is willing to turn from sin he will be surprised to see how the light will come in!

I remember one night when the Bible was the driest and darkest book in the universe to me. The next day it became entirely different. I thought I had the key to it. I had been born of the Spirit. But before I knew anything of the mind of God I had to give up my sin. I believe God meets every soul on the spot of self surrender; and when they are willing to let Him guide and lead. The trouble with many sceptics is their self-conceit. They know more than the Almighty! and they do not come in a teachable spirit. But the moment a man comes in a receptive spirit he is blessed; for "If any of you lack wisdom, let him ask of God, that giveth to all men liberally, and upbraideth not; and it shall be given him" (James i. 5).

CHAPTER V.

A DIVINE SAVIOUR.

"Thou art THE CHRIST, the Son of the living God."
(MATTHEW xvi. 1. JOHN vi. 69.)

WE meet with a certain class of Enquirers who do not believe in the Divinity of Christ. There are many passages that will give light on this subject.

In 1 Corinthians xv. 47, we are told: "The first man is of the earth earthy: the second man is the Lord from heaven."

In 1 John v. 20: "We know that the Son of God is come, and hath given us an understanding, that we may know Him that is true; and we are in Him that is true, even in His Son Jesus Christ. This is the true God, and eternal life."

Again in John xvii. 3: "And this is life eternal, that they might know Thee, the only true God; and Jesus Christ, whom Thou hast sent."

And then, in Mark xiv. 60: "The high priest stood up in the midst, and asked Jesus, saying, Answerest Thou nothing? What is it which these witness against thee? But He held His peace, and answered nothing. Again the high priest asked Him, and said unto Him, Art Thou the Christ, the Son of the Blessed? And Jesus said, I am: and ye shall see the Son of Man sitting on the right hand of power, and coming in the clouds of heaven. Then the high priest rent his clothes, and saith, What need we any further witnesses? Ye have heard the blasphemy: what think ye? And they all condemned Him to be guilty of death."

Now what brought me to believe in the Divinity of Christ was this: I did not know where to place Christ, or what to do with Him, if He were not divine. When I was a boy I thought that He was a good man like Moses, Joseph, or Abraham. I even thought that He was the best man who had ever lived on the earth. But I found that Christ had a higher claim. He claimed to be God-Man, to be divine; to have come from heaven. He said: "Before Abraham was I am" (John viii. 58). I could not understand this; and I was driven to the conclusion—and I challenge any candid man to deny the inference, or meet the argument—that Jesus Christ is either an impostor or deceiver, or He is the God-Man—God manifest in the flesh. And for these reasons. The first commandment is, "Thou shalt have no other gods before Me" (Exod. xx. 2). Look at the millions throughout Christendom who worship Jesus Christ as God. If Christ be not God this is idolatry. We are all guilty of breaking the first commandment if Jesus Christ were mere man—if He were a created being, and not what He claims to be.

Some people, who do not admit His divinity, say that He was the best man who ever lived; but if He were not Divine, for that very reason He ought not to be reckoned a good man, for He laid claim to an honor and dignity to which these very people declare He had no right or title. That would rank Him as a deceiver.

Others say that He thought He was divine, but that He was deceived. As if Jesus Christ were carried away by a delusion and deception, and thought that He was more than He was! I could not conceive of a lower idea of Jesus Christ than that. This would not only make Him out an impostor; but that He was out of His mind, and that He did not know who He was, or where He came from. Now if Jesus Christ was not what He claimed to be, the Saviour of the world; and if He did not come from heaven, He was a gross deceiver.

But how can any one read the life of Jesus Christ and make Him out a deceiver? A man has generally some motive for being an impostor. What was Christ's motive? He knew that the course He was pursuing would conduct Him to the cross; that His name would be cast out as vile; and that many of His followers would be called upon to lay down their lives for His sake. Nearly every one of the apostles were martyrs; and they were considered as off-scouring and refuse in the midst of the people. If a man is an impostor, he has a motive at the back of his hypocrisy. But what was Christ's object? The record is that "He went about doing good." This is not the work of an impostor. Do not let the enemy of your soul deceive you.

In John v. 21 we read: "For as the Father raiseth up the dead, and quickeneth them; even so the Son quickeneth whom He will. For the Father judgeth no man, but hath committed all judgment unto the Son: that all men should honor the Son, even as they honor the Father. He that honoureth not the Son, honoureth not the Father which hath sent Him."

Now, notice: by the Jewish law if a man were a blasphemer he was to be put to death; and supposing Christ to be merely human if this be not blasphemy I do not know where you will find it. "He that honoureth not the Son, honoureth not the Father." That is downright blasphemy if Christ be not divine. If Moses, or Elijah, or Elisha, or any other mortal had said, "You must honour me as you honour God;" and had put himself on a level with God, it would have been downright blasphemy.

The Jews put Christ to death because they said that He was not what He claimed to be. It was on that testimony He was put under oath. The high priest said: "I adjure Thee by the living God, that Thou tell us whether Thou be the Christ, the Son of God" (Matt. xxvi. 63). And when the Jews came round Him and said, "How long dost Thou make us to doubt? If Thou be the Christ tell us plainly." Jesus said, "I and My Father are one." Then the Jews took up stones again to stone Him. (John x. 24—33.) They said they did not want to hear more, for that was blasphemy. It was for declaring Himself to be the Son of God that He was condemned and put to death. (Matt. xxvi. 63—66).

Now if Jesus Christ were mere man the Jews did right, according to their law, in putting Him to death. In Leviticus xxiv. 16, we read: "And he that blasphemeth the name of the Lord, he shall surely be put to death, and all the congregation shall certainly stone him: as well the stranger, as he that is born in the land, when he blasphemeth the name of the Lord, shall be put to death."

This law obliged them to put to death every one who blasphemed. It was making the statement that He was divine that cost Him His life; and by the Mosaic law He ought to have suffered the death penalty. In John xvi. 15, Christ says, "All things that the Father hath are Mine: therefore said I, that He shall take of Mine, and shall show it unto you." How could He be merely a good man and use language as that?

No doubt has ever entered my mind on the point since I was converted.

A notorious sinner was once asked how he could prove the divinity of Christ. His answer was, "Why, He has saved me; and that is a pretty good proof, is it not?"

An infidel on one occasion said to me, "I have been studying the life of John the Baptist, Mr. Moody. Why don't you preach him? He was a greater character than Christ. You would do a greater work." I said to him, "My friend, *you* preach John the Baptist; and I will follow you and preach Christ: and we will see who will do the most good." "You will do the most good," he said, "because the people are so superstitious." Ah! John was beheaded; and his disciples begged his body and buried it: but Christ has risen from the dead; He has "ascended on high; He has led captivity captive; and received gifts for men." Ps. lxviii. 18.)

Our Christ LIVES. Many people have not found out that Christ has risen from the grave. They worship a dead Saviour, like Mary, who said, "They have taken away my Lord; and I know not where they have laid Him." (John xx. 13.) That is the trouble with those who doubt the divinity of our Lord.

Then look at Matthew xviii. 20. "Where two or three are gathered together in My name, there am I in the midst of them." "THERE AM I." Well now, if He is a mere man, how can He be there? All these are strong passages.

Again in Matthew xxviii. 18. "And Jesus came and spake unto them, saying, "All power is given unto Me in heaven and in earth." Could He be a mere man and talk in that way? "All power is given unto Me in heaven and in earth!"

Then again in Matthew xxviii. 20. "Teaching them to observe all things whatsoever I have commanded you; and, lo, I am with you alway, even unto the end of the world." If He were mere man, how could He be with us? Yet He says, "I am with you alway, even unto the end of the world!"

Then again in Mark ii. 7. "Why doth this Man thus speak blasphemies? who can forgive sins but God only? And immediately when Jesus perceived in His Spirit that they reasoned within themselves, He said unto them, Why reason ye these things in your hearts? Whether is it easier to say to the sick of the palsy, Thy sins be forgiven thee, or to say, Arise, and take up thy bed and walk?"

Some men will meet you and say, "Did not Elisha also raise the dead?" Notice that in the rare instances in which men have raised the dead, they did it by the power of God. They called on God to do it. But when Christ was on earth He did not call upon the Father to bring the dead to life, When He went to the house of Jairus He said, "Damsel, *I* say unto thee, Arise." (Mark v. 41.)

He had power to impart life. When they were carrying the young man out of Nain He had compassion on the widowed mother and came and touched the bier and said, "Young man, *I* say unto thee, Arise." (Luke vii. 14.)

He spake; and the dead arose.

And when He raised Lazarus He called with a loud voice, "Lazarus, come forth!" (John xi. 43.) And Lazarus heard, and came forth.

Some one has said, It was a good thing that Lazarus was mentioned by name, or all the dead within the sound of Christ's voice would immediately have risen.

In John v. 25, Jesus says: "Verily, verily, I say unto you, The hour is coming, and now is, when the dead shall hear the voice of the Son of God; and they that hear shall live." What blasphemy would this have been, had He not been divine! The proof is overwhelming, if you will but examine the Word of God.

And then another thing—no good man except Jesus Christ has ever allowed anybody to worship him. When this was done He never rebuked the worshiper. In John ix. 38, we read that when the blind man was found by Christ he said, "Lord, I believe. And he worshiped Him." The Lord did not rebuke him.

Then again, Revelation xxii. 6, runs thus: "And he said unto me, These things are faithful and true; and the Lord God of the holy prophets sent His angel to show unto His servants the things which must shortly be done. Behold, I come quickly: blessed is he that keepeth the sayings of the prophecy of this book. And I John saw these things and heard them. And when I had heard and seen, I fell down to worship before the feet of the angel which showed me these things. Then saith He unto me, See thou do it not; for I am thy fellow-servant and of thy brethren the prophets, and of them which keep the sayings of this book: *worship God.*"

We see here that even that angel would not allow John to worship him. Even an angel from heaven! And if Gabriel came down here from the presence of God it would be a sin to worship him, or any seraph, or any cherub, or Michael, or any archangel.

"Worship God!" And if Jesus Chist were not God manifest in the flesh we are guilty of idolatry in worshiping Him. In Matthew xiv. 33, we read: "Then they that were in the ship came and *worshiped* Him, saying, Of a truth Thou art the Son of God." He did not rebuke them.

And in Matthew viii. 2, we also read: "And, behold, there came a leper and *worshiped* Him, saying, Lord, if Thou wilt, Thou canst make me clean."

In Matthew xv. 25: "Then came she, and *worshiped* Him, saying, Lord, help me!"

There are many other passages; but I give these as sufficient in my opinion to prove beyond any doubt the Divinity of our Lord.

In the 14th chapter of Acts we are told the heathen of Lystra came with garlands and would have done sacrifice to Paul and Barnabas because they had cured an impotent man; but the evangelists rent their clothes and told these Lystrans that they were but men, and not to be worshipped; as if it were a great sin. And if Jesus Christ is a mere man, we are all guilty of a great sin in worshipping Him.

But if He is, as we believe, the only-begotten and well-beloved Son of God, let us yield to His claims upon us; let us rest on His all-atoning work, and go forth to serve Him all the days of our life.

CHAPTER VI.

REPENTANCE AND RESTITUTION.

"God commandeth all men everywhere to repent."—Acts xvii. 30.

Repentance is one of the fundamental doctrines of the Bible. Yet I believe it is one of those truths that many people little understand at the present day. There are more people to-day in the mist and darkness about Repentance, Regeneration, the Atonement, and such-like fundamental truths, than perhaps on any other doctrines. Yet from our earliest years we have heard about them. If I were to ask for a definition of Repentance, a great many would give a very strange and false idea of it.

A man is not prepared to believe or to receive the Gospel, unless he is ready to repent of his sins and turn from them. Until John the Baptist met Christ, he had but one text, "Repent ye; for the kingdom of heaven is at hand" (Matt. iii. 2). But if he had continued to say this, and had stopped there without pointing the people to Christ the Lamb of God, he would not have accomplished much.

When Christ came, He took up the same wilderness cry, "Repent; for the kingdom of heaven is at hand" (Matt. iv. 17). And when our Lord sent out His disciples, it was with the same message, "that men should repent" (Mark vi. 12). After He had been glorified, and when the Holy Ghost came down, we find Peter on the day of Pentecost raising the same cry, "Repent!" It was this preaching—Repent, and believe the Gospel—that wrought such marvellous results then. (Acts ii. 38—47). And we find that, when Paul went to

Athens, he uttered the same cry, "*Now* God commandeth *all men, everywhere*, to repent" (Acts xvii. 30).

Before I speak of what Repentance *is*, let me briefly say what it *is not*. Repentance is not *fear*. Many people have confounded the two. They think they have to be alarmed and terrified; and they are waiting for some kind of fear to come down upon them. But multitudes become alarmed who do not really repent. You have heard of men at sea during a terrible storm. Perhaps they have been very profane men; but when the danger came they suddenly grew quiet, and began to cry to God for mercy. Yet you would not say they repented. When the storm had passed away, they went on swearing the same as before. You might think that the king of Egypt repented when God sent the terrible plagues upon him and his land. But it was not repentance at all. The moment God's hand was removed Pharaoh's heart was harder than ever. He did not turn from a single sin; he was the same man. So that there was no true repentance there.

Often, when death comes into a family, it looks as if the event would be sanctified to the conversion of all who are in the house. Yet in six months' time all may be forgotten. Some who read this have perhaps passed through that experience. When God's hand was heavy upon them it looked as if they were going to repent; but the trial has been removed—and lo and behold, the impression has all gone.

Then again, Repentance is not *feeling*. I find a great many people are waiting for a certain kind of feeling to come. They would like to turn to God; but think they cannot do it until this feeling comes. When I was in Baltimore I used to preach every Sunday in the Penitentiary to nine hundred convicts. There was hardly a man there who did not feel miserable enough: they had plenty of feeling. For the first week or ten days of their imprisonment many of them cried half the time. Yet, when they were released, most of them would go right back to their old ways. The truth was, that they felt very bad because they had got caught; that was all. So you have seen a man in the time of trial show a good deal of feeling: but very often it is only because he has got into trouble; not because he has committed sin, or because his conscience tells him he has done evil in the sight of God. It seems as if the trial were going to result in true repentance; but the feeling too often passes away.

Once again, Repentance is not *fasting and afflicting the body*. A man may fast for weeks and months and years, and yet not repent of one sin. Neither is it *remorse*. Judas had terrible remorse—enough to make him go and hang himself; but that was not repentance. I believe if he had gone to his Lord, fallen on his face, and confessed his sin, he would have been forgiven. Instead of this he went to the priests, and then put an end to his life. A man may do all sorts of penance—but there is no true repentance in that. Put that down in your mind. You cannot meet the claims of God by offering the fruit of your body for the sin of your soul. Away with such a delusion!

Repentance is not *conviction of sin*. That may sound strange to some. I have seen men under such deep conviction of sin that they could not sleep at night; they could not enjoy a single meal. They went on for months in this state; and yet they were not converted; they did not truly repent. Do not confound conviction of sin with Repentance.

Neither is *praying*—Repentance. That too may sound strange. Many people, when they become anxious about their soul's salvation, say, "I will pray, and read the Bible;" and they think that will bring about the desired effect. But it will not do it. You may read the Bible and cry to God a great deal, and yet never repent. Many people cry loudly to God, and yet do not repent.

Another thing: it is not *breaking off some one sin.* A great many people make that mistake. A man who has been a drunkard signs the pledge, and stops drinking. Breaking off one sin is not Repentance. Forsaking one vice is like breaking off one limb of a tree, when the whole tree has to come down. A profane man stops swearing; very good: but if he does not break off *from every sin* it is not Repentance—it is not the work of God in the soul. When God works He hews down the whole tree. He wants to have a man turn from every sin. Supposing I am in a vessel out at sea, and I find the ship leaks in three or four places. I may go and stop up one hole; yet down goes the vessel. Or suppose I am wounded in three or four places, and I get a remedy for one wound: if the other two or three wounds are neglected, my life will soon be gone. True Repentance is not merely breaking off this or that particular sin.

Well then, you will ask, what is Repentance? I will give you a good definition: it is "right about face!" In the Irish language the word "Repentance" means even more than "right about face!" It implies that a man who has been walking in one direction has not only faced about, but is actually walking in an exactly contrary direction. "Turn ye, turn ye; for why will ye die?" A man may have little feeling or much feeling; but if he do not turn away from sin, God will not have mercy on him. Repentance has also been described as "a change of mind." For instance, there is the parable told by Christ: "A certain man had two sons; and he came to the first, and said, Son, go work to-day in my vineyard. He answered and said, I will not" (Matt. xxi. 28, 29). After he had said "I will not" he thought over it, and changed his mind. Perhaps he may have said to himself, "I did not speak very respectfully to my father. He asked me to go and work, and I told him I would not go. I think I was wrong." But suppose he had only said this, and still had not gone, he would not have repented. He was not only convinced that he was wrong; but he went off into the fields, hoeing, or mowing or whatever it was. That is Christ's definition of repentance. If a man says, "By the grace of God I will forsake my sin, and do His will," that is Repentance—a turning right about.

Some one has said, man is born with his face turned away from God. When he truly repents he is turned right around towards God; he leaves his old life.

Can a man at once repent? Certainly he can. It does not take a long while to turn around. It does not take a man six months to change his mind. There was a vessel that went down some time ago on the Newfoundland coast. As she was bearing towards the shore, there was a moment when the captain could have given orders to reverse the engines and turn back. If the engines had been reversed then, the ship would have been saved. But there was a moment when it was too late. So there is a moment, I believe, in every man's life when he can halt and say, "By the grace of God I will go no further towards death and ruin. I repent of my sins and turn from them." You may say you have not got feeling enough; but if you are convinced that you are on the wrong road, turn right about, and say, "I will no longer go on in the way of rebellion and sin as I have done." Just then, when you are willing to turn towards God, salvation may be yours.

I find that every case of conversion recorded in the Bible was instantaneous. Repentance and faith came very suddenly. The moment a man made up his mind, God gave him the power. God does not ask any man to do what he has not the power to do. He would not "command all men everywhere to repent" (Acts xvii. 30) if they were not able to do so. Man has no one to blame but himself if he does not repent and believe the Gospel. One of the leading ministers of the Gospel in Ohio wrote me a letter some time ago describing his conversion; it very forcibly illustrates this point of instantaneous decision. He said:

"I was nineteen years old, and was reading law with a Christian lawyer in Vermont. One afternoon when he was away from home, his good wife said to me as I came into the house, 'I want you to go to class-meeting with me to-night and become a Christian, so that you can conduct family worship while my husband is away.' 'Well, I'll do it,' I said, without any thought. When I came into the house again she asked me if I was honest in what I had said. I replied, 'Yes, so far as going to meeting with you is concerned; that is only courteous.'

"I went with her to the class-meeting, as I had often done before. About a dozen persons were present in a little schoolhouse. The leader had spoken to all in the room but myself and two others. He was speaking to the person next me, when the thought occurred to me: he will ask me if I have anything to say. I said to myself: I have decided to be a Christian sometime; why not begin now? In less time than a minute after these thoughts had passed through my mind he said, speaking to me familiarly—for he knew me very well—'Brother Charles, have you anything to say? I replied, with perfect coolness, 'Yes, sir. I have just decided, within the last thirty seconds, that I will begin a Christian life, and would like to have you pray for me.'

"My coolness staggered him; I think he almost doubted my sincerity. He said very little, but passed on and spoke to the other two. After a few general remarks, he turned to me and said, 'Brother Charles, will you close the meeting with prayer?' He knew I had never prayed in public. Up to this moment I had no feeling. It was purely a business transaction. My first thought was: I cannot pray, and I will ask him to excuse me. My second was: I have said I will begin a Christian life; and this is a part of it. So I said, 'Let us pray.' And somewhere between the time I started to kneel and the time my knees struck the floor the Lord converted my soul.

"The first words I said were, 'Glory to God!' What I said after that I do not know, and it does not matter, for my soul was too full to say much but 'Glory!' From that hour the devil has never dared to challenge my conversion. To Christ be all the praise."

Many people are waiting, they cannot exactly tell for what, but for some sort of miraculous feeling to come stealing over them—some mysterious kind of faith. I was speaking to a man some years ago, and he always had one answer to give me. For five years I tried to win him to Christ, and every year he said, "It has not 'struck me' yet." "Man, what do you mean? What has not struck you?" "Well," he said, "I am not going to become a Christian until it strikes me; and it has not struck me yet. I do not see it in the way you see it." "But don't you know you are a sinner?" "Yes, I know I am a sinner." "Well, don't you know that God wants to have mercy on you—that there is forgiveness with God? He wants you to repent and come to Him." "Yes, I know that; but—it has not struck me yet." He always fell back on that. Poor man! he went down to his grave in a state of indecision. Sixty long years God gave him to repent; and all he had to say at the end of those years was that it "had not struck him yet."

Is any reader waiting for some strange feeling—you do not know what? Nowhere in the Bible is a man told to wait; God is commanding you *now* to repent.

Do you think God can forgive a man when he does not want to be forgiven? Would he be happy if God forgave him in this state of mind? Why, if a man went into the kingdom of God without repentance, heaven would be hell to him. Heaven is a prepared place for a prepared people. If your boy has done wrong, and will not repent, you cannot forgive him. You would be doing him an injustice. Suppose he goes to your desk, and steals $10, and squanders it. When you come home your servant tells you what your boy has done. You ask if it is true, and he denies it. But at last you have certain proof. Even when he finds he cannot deny it any longer, he will not confess the sin, but says he will do it again the first chance he gets. Would you say to him, "Well, I forgive you," and leave the matter there? No! Yet people say that God is going to save all men, whether they repent or not—drunkards, thieves, harlots, whoremongers, it makes no difference. "God is so merciful," they say. Dear friend, do not be deceived by the god of this world. Where there is true repentance and a turning from sin unto God, He will meet and bless you; but He never blesses until there is sincere repentance.

David made a woful mistake in this respect with his rebellious son, Absalom. He could not have done his son a greater injustice than to forgive him when his heart was unchanged. There could be no true reconcilliation between them when there was no repentance. But God does not make these mistakes. David got into trouble on account of his error of judgment. His son soon drove his father from the throne.

Speaking on repentance, Dr. Brooks, of St. Louis, well remarks: "Repentance, strictly speaking, means a 'change of mind or purpose;' consequently it is the judgment which the sinner pronounces upon himself, in view of the love of God displayed in the death of Christ, connected with the abandonment of all confidence in himself and with trust in the only Saviour of sinners. Saving repentance and saving faith always go together; and you need not be worried about repentance if you will believe."

"Some people are no sure that they have 'repented enough.' If you mean by this that you must repent in order to incline God to be merciful to you, the sooner you give over such repentance the better. God is already merciful, as He has fully shown at the Cross of Calvary; and it is a grievous dishonor to His heart of love if you think that your tears and anguish will move Him, 'not knowing that the goodness of God leadeth thee to repentance.' It is not your badness, therefore, but His goodness that leads to repentance; hence the true way to repent is to believe on the Lord Jesus Christ, 'who was delivered for our offences, and was raised again for our justification.'"

Another thing. If there is true repentance it will bring forth fruit. If we have done wrong to any one we should never ask God to forgive us, until we are willing to make restitution. If I have done any man a great injustice and can make it good, I need not ask God to forgive me until I am willing to make it good. Suppose I have taken something that does not belong to me. I have no right to expect forgiveness until I make restitution.

I remember preaching in one of our large cities, when a fine-looking man came up to me at the close. He was in great distress of mind. "The fact is," he said, "I am a defaulter. I have taken money that belonged to my employers. How can I become a Christian without restoring it?" "Have you got the money?" He told me he had not got it all. He had taken about $1,500, and he still had about $900. He said, "Could I not take that money and go into business, and make enough to pay them back?" I told him that was a delusion of Satan;

that he could not expect to prosper on stolen money; that he should restore all he had, and go and ask his employers to have mercy upon him and forgive him. "But they will put me in prison," he said: "cannot you give me any help?" "No, you must restore the money before you can expect to get any help from God." "It is pretty hard," he said. "Yes, it is hard; but the great mistake was in doing the wrong at first."

His burden became so heavy that it got to be insupportable. He handed me the money—950 dollars and some cents—and asked me to take it back to his employers. The next evening the two employers and myself met in a side room of the church. I laid the money down, and informed them it was from one of their *employes*. I told them the story, and said he wanted mercy from them, not justice. The tears trickled down the cheeks of these two men, and they said, "Forgive him! Yes, we will be glad to forgive him." I went down stairs and brought him up. After he had confessed his guilt and been forgiven, we all got down on our knees and had a blessed prayer-meeting. God met us and blessed us there.

There was a friend of mine who some time ago had come to Christ and wished to consecrate himself and his wealth to God. He had formerly had transactions with the government, and had taken advantage of them. This thing came up when he was converted, and his conscience troubled him. He said, "I want to consecrate my wealth, but it seems as if God will not take it." He had a terrible struggle; his conscience kept rising up and smiting him. At last he drew a check for $1,500 and sent it to the United States Treasury. He told me he received such a blessing when he had done it. That was bringing forth "fruits meet for repentance." I believe a great many men are crying to God for light; and they are not getting it because they are not honest.

I was once preaching, and a man came to me who was only thirty-two years old, but whose hair was very grey. He said, "I want you to notice that my hair is grey, and I am only thirty-two years old. For twelve years I have carried a great burden." "Well," I said, "what is it?" He looked around as if afraid some one would hear him. "Well," he answered, "my father died and left my mother with the county newspaper, and left her only that: that was all she had. After he died the paper began to waste away; and I saw my mother was fast sinking into a state of need. The building and the paper were insured for a thousand dollars, and when I was twenty years old I set fire to the building, and obtained the thousand dollars, and gave it to my mother. For twelve years that sin has been haunting me. I have tried to drown it by indulgence in pleasure and sin; I have cursed God; I have gone into infidelity; I have tried to make out that the Bible is not true; I have done everything I could: but all these years I have been tormented." I said, "There is a way out of that." He inquired "How?" I said, "Make restitution. Let us sit down and calculate the interest, and then you pay the Company the money." It would have done you good to see that man's face light up when he found there was mercy for him. He said he would be glad to pay back the money and interest if he could only be forgiven.

There are men to-day who are in darkness and bondage because they are not willing to turn from their sins and confess them; and I do not know how a man can hope to be forgiven if he is not willing to confess his sins.

Bear in mind that *now* is the only day of mercy you will ever have. You can repent now, and have the awful record blotted out. God waits to forgive you; He is seeking to bring you to Himself. But I think the Bible teaches clearly that there is *no repentance after this life.* There are some who tell you of the possibility of repentance in the grave; but I do not find that in Scripture. I have looked my Bible over very carefully, and I cannot find that a man will have another opportunity of being saved.

Why should he ask for any more time? You have time enough to repent now. You can turn from your sins this moment if you will. God says: "I have no pleasure in the death of him that dieth; wherefore turn, and live ye" (Ezek. xviii. 32).

Christ said, He "came not to call the righteous, but sinners to repentance." Are you a sinner? Then the call to repent is addressed to you. Take your place in the dust at the Saviour's feet, and acknowledge your guilt. Say, like the publican of old, "God be merciful to me a sinner!" and see how quickly He will pardon and bless you. He will even justify you and reckon you as righteous, by virtue of the righteousness of Him who bore your sins in His own body on the Cross.

There are some perhaps who think themselves righteous; and that, therefore, there is no need for them to repent and believe the Gospel. They are like the Pharisee in the parable, who thanked God that he was not as other men—"extortioners, unjust, adulterers, or even as this publican;" and who went on to say, "I fast twice a week; I give tithes of all I possess." What is the judgment about such self-righteous persons? "I tell you this man [the poor, contrite, repenting publican] went down to his house justified rather than the other" (Luke xviii. 11—14). "There is none righteous; no, not one." "All have sinned, and come short of the glory of God" (Rom. iii. 10, 23). Let no one say *he* does not need to repent. Let each one take his true place—that of a sinner; then God will lift him up to the place of forgiveness and justification. "Whosoever exalteth himself shall be abased; and he that humbleth himself shall be exalted" (Luke xiv. 11).

Wherever God sees true repentance in the heart He meets that soul.

I was in Colorado, preaching the gospel some time ago, and I heard something that touched my heart very much. The governor of the State was passing through the prison, and in one cell he found a boy who had his window full of flowers, that seemed to have been watched with very tender care. The governor looked at the prisoner, and then at the flowers, and asked whose they were, "These are my flowers," said the poor convict. "Are you fond of flowers?" "Yes, sir." "How long have you been here?" He told him so many years: he was in for a long sentence. The governor was surprised to find him so fond of the flowers, and he said, "Can you tell me why you like these flowers so much?" With much emotion he replied, "While my mother was alive she thought a good deal of flowers; and when I came here I thought if I had these they would remind me of mother." The governor was so pleased that he said, "Well, young man, if you think so much of your mother I think you will appreciate your liberty," and he pardoned him then and there.

When God finds that beautiful flower of true repentance springing up in a man's heart, then salvation comes to that man.

CHAPTER VII.

ASSURANCE OF SALVATION.

These things have I written unto you that believe on the name of the Son of God; that ye may know that ye have eternal life, and that ye may believe on the name of the Son of God."

(1 JOHN V. 13.)

THERE are two classes who ought not to have Assurance. First: those who are in the Church, but who are not converted, having never been born of the Spirit. Second: those are not willing to do God's will; who are not ready to take the place that God has mapped out for them, but want to fill some other place.

Some one will ask "Have all God's people Assurance?" No; I think a good many of God's dear people have no Assurance; but it is the privilege of every child of God to have beyond doubt a knowledge of his own salvation. No man is fit for God's service who is filled with doubts. If a man is not sure of his own salvation, how can he help any one else into the kingdom of God? If I seem in danger of drowning and do not know whether I shall ever reach the shore, I cannot assist another. I must first get on the solid rock myself; and then I can lend my brother a helping hand. If being myself blind I were to tell another blind man how to get sight, he might reply, "First get healed yourself; and then you can tell me." I recently met with a young man who was a Christian; but he had not attained to victory over sin. He was in terrible darkness. Such an one is not fit to work for God, because he has besetting sins; and he has not the victory over his doubts, because he has not the victory over his sins.

None will have time or heart to work for God, who are not assured as to their own salvation. They have as much as they can attend to; and being themselves burdened with doubts, they cannot help others to carry their burdens. There is no rest, joy, or peace—no liberty, nor power—where doubts and uncertainty exist.

Now it seems as if there are three wiles of Satan against which we ought to be on our guard. In the first place he moves all his kingdom to keep us away from Christ; then he devotes himself to get us into "Doubting Castle:" but if we have, in spite of him, a clear ringing witness for the Son of God, he will do all he can to blacken our characters and belie our testimony.

Some seem to think that it is presumption not to have doubts: but doubt is very dishonoring to God. If any one were to say that they had known a person for thirty years and yet doubted him, it would not be very creditable: and when we have known God for ten, twenty or thirty years does it not reflect on His veracity to doubt Him?

Could Paul and the early Christians and martyrs have gone through what they did if they had been filled with doubts, and had not known whether they were going to heaven or to perdition after they had been burned at the stake? They must have had ASSURANCE.

Mr. Spurgeon says: "I never heard of a stork that when it met with a fir tree demurred as to its right to build its nest there; and I never heard of a coney yet that questioned whether it had a permit to run into the rock. Why, these creatures would soon perish if they were always doubting and fearing as to whether they had a right to use providential provisions.

"The stork says to himself, 'Ah, here is a fir tree:' he consults with his mate, 'Will this do for the nest in which we may rear our young?' 'Aye,' says she; and they gather the materials, and arrange them. There is never any deliberation, 'May we build here?' but they bring their sticks and make their nest.

"The wild goat on the crag does not say, 'Have I a right here?' No, he must be somewhere: and there is a crag which exactly suits him; and he springs upon it.

"Yet, though these dumb creatures know the provision of their God, the sinner does not recognize the provision of his Saviour. He quibbles and questions, 'May I?' and 'I am afraid it is not for me;' and 'I think it cannot be meant for me;' and 'I am afraid it is too good to be true.'

"And yet nobody ever said to the stork, 'Whosoever buildeth on this fir tree shall never have his nest pulled down.' No inspired word has ever said to the coney, 'Whosoever runs into this rock cleft shall never be driven out of it." If it had been so it would make assurance doubly sure.

"And yet here is Christ provided for sinners, just the sort of a Saviour sinners need; and the encouragement is added, 'Him that cometh unto Me I will in no wise cast out;' 'Whosoever will, let him take the water of life freely.' "

Now let us come to the Word. John tells us in his Gospel what Christ did for us on earth. In his Epistle He tells us what He is doing for us in heaven as our Advocate. In his Gospel there are only two chapters in which the word "believe" does not occur. With these two exceptions, every chapter in John is "Believe! *Believe!!* BELIEVE!!!" He tells us in xx. 31, "But these are written, that ye might believe that Jesus is the Christ, the son of God, and that, believing, ye might have life through His name. That is the purpose for which he wrote the Gospel—"that we might believe that Jesus is the Christ, the Son of God: and that, believing, we might have life through His name" (John xx. 31).

Turn to 1 John v. 13, he there tells us why he wrote this Epistle: "These things have I written unto you that believe on the name of the Son of God." Notice to whom he writes it: "You that believe on the name of the Son of God; that ye may know that ye have eternal life, and that ye may believe on the name of the Son of God." There are only five short chapters in this first Epistle, and the word "know" occurs over forty times. It is "*Know!* KNOW!! KNOW!!!" The *Key* to it is KNOW! and all through the Epistle there rings out the refrain—"that we might know that we have eternal life."

I went twelve hundred miles down the Mississippi in the spring some years ago; and every evening, just as the sun went down, you might have seen men, and sometimes women, riding up to the banks of the river on either side on mules or horses, and sometimes coming on foot, for the purpose of lighting up the Government lights; and all down that mighty river there were landmarks which guided the pilots in their dangerous navigation. Now God has given us lights or landmarks to tell us whether we are His children or not; and what we need to do is to examine the tokens He has given us.

In the third chapter of John's first Epistle there are five things worth knowing.

In the fifth verse we read the first: "And ye *know* that He was manifiested to take away our sins; and in Him is no sin." Not what I have done, but what HE has done. Has He failed in His mission? Is He not able to do what He came for? Did ever any heaven-sent man fail yet? and could God's own Son fail? HE WAS MANIFESTED TO TAKE AWAY OUR SINS.

Again, in the nineteenth verse, the second thing worth knowing: "And hereby *we know* that we are of the truth, and shall *assure* our hearts before Him." WE KNOW that we are of THE TRUTH. And if the truth make us free, we shall be free indeed. "If the Son therefore shall make you free, ye shall be free indeed." (John viii. 36.)

The third thing worth knowing is in the fourteenth verse, "*We know* that we have passed from death unto life, because we love the brethren." The natural man does not like godly people, nor does he care to be in their company. "He that loveth not his brother abideth in death." He has no spiritual life.

The fourth thing worth knowing we find in verse twenty-four: "And he that keepeth His commandments dwelleth in Him, and He in him. And hereby *we know* that He abideth in us, by the Spirit which He hath given us. We can tell what kind of Spirit we have if we possess the Spirit of Christ—a Christ-like spirit—not the same in degree, but the same in kind. If I am meek, gentle, and forgiving; if I have a spirit filled with peace and joy; if I am long-suffering and gentle, like the Son of God—that is a test: and in that way we are to tell whether we have eternal life or not.

The fifth thing worth knowing, and the best of all, is "Beloved, *now*." Notice the word "Now." It does not say when you come to die. "Beloved, *now* are we the sons of God; and it doth not yet appear what we shall be: but *we know* that, when He shall appear, we shall be like Him; for we shall see Him as He is" (*v.* 2).

But some will say, "Well, I believe all that; but then I have sinned since I became a Christian." Is there a man or a woman on the face of the earth who has not sinned since becoming a Christian? Not one! There never has been, and never will be, a soul on this earth who has not sinned, or who will not sin, at some time of their Christian experience. But God has made provision for believers' sins. *We* are not to make provision for them; but God has. Bear that in mind.

Turn to 1 John ii. 1: "My little children, these things write I unto you, that ye sin not. And if any man sin, we have an Advocate with the Father, Jesus Christ the righteous." He is here writing to the righteous. "If any man sin, *we*"—John put himself in—"we have an Advocate with the Father, Jesus Christ the righteous." What an Advocate! He attends to our interests at the very best place—the throne of God. He said, "Nevertheless, I tell you the truth; it is expedient for you that I go away" (John xvi. 7). He went away to become our High Priest, and also our Advocate. He has had some hard cases to plead; but he has never lost one: and if you entrust your immortal interests to Him, He will "present you faultless before the presence of His glory with exceeding joy" (Jude 24).

The past sins of Christians are all forgiven as soon as they are confessed; and they are never to be mentioned. That is a question which is not to be opened up again. If our sins have been put away, that is the end of them. They are not to be remembered; and God will not mention them any more. This is very plain. Suppose I have a son who, while I am from home, does wrong. When I go home he throws his arms around my neck and says, "Papa, I did what you told me not to do. I am very sorry. Do forgive me." I say: "Yes, my son," and kiss him. He wipes away his tears, and goes off rejoicing.

But the next day he says: "Papa, I wish you would forgive me for the wrong I did yesterday." I should say: "Why, my son, that thing is settled; and I don't want it mentioned again." "But I wish you would forgive me: it would help me to hear you say, 'I forgive you.'" Would that be honoring me? Would it not grieve me to have my boy doubt me? But to gratify him I say again, "I forgive you, my son."

And if, the next day, he were again to bring up that old sin, and ask forgiveness, would not that grieve me to the heart? And so, my dear reader, if God has forgiven us, never let us mention the past. Let us forget those things which are behind, and reach forth unto those which are before, and press toward the mark for the prize of the high calling of God in Christ Jesus. Let the sins of the past go; for "If we confess our sins, He is faithful and just to forgive us our sins, and to cleanse us from all unrighteousness" (1 John i. 9).

And let me say that this principle is recognized in courts of justice. A case came up in the courts of a country—I won't say where—in which a man had had trouble with his wife; but he forgave her, and then afterwards brought her into court. And, when it was known that he had forgiven her, the judge said that the thing was settled. The judge recognized the soundness of the principle, that if a sin were once forgiven there was an end of it. And do you think the Judge of all the earth will forgive you and me, and open the question again? Our sins are gone for time and eternity, if God forgives; and what we have to do is to confess and forsake our sins.

Again in 2 Corinthians xiii. 5: "Examine yourselves whether ye be in the faith; prove your own selves. Know ye not your own selves, how that Jesus Christ is in you, except ye be reprobates?" Now examine yourselves. Try your religion. Put it to the test. Can you forgive an enemy? That is a good way to know if you are a child of God. Can you forgive an injury, or take an affront, as Christ did? Can you be censured for doing well, and not murmur? Can you be misjudged and misrepresented, and yet keep a Christ-like spirit?

Another good test is to read Galatians v., and notice the fruits of the Spirit; and see if you have them. "The fruit of the Spirit is love, joy, peace, long suffering, gentleness, goodness faith, meekness, temperance: against such there is no law." If I have the fruits of the Spirit I must have the Spirit. I could not have the fruits without the Spirit any more than there could be an orange without the tree. And Christ says: "Ye shall know them by their fruits;" "for the tree is known by his fruits." Make the tree good, and the fruit will be good. The only way to get the fruit is to have the Spirit. That is the way to examine ourselves whether we are the children of God.

Then there is another very striking passage. In Romans viii. 9, Paul says: "Now, if any man have not the Spirit of Christ, he is none of His." That ought to settle the question, even though one may have gone through all the external forms that are considered necessary by some to constitute a member of a Church. Read Paul's life, and put yours alongside of it. If your life resembles his, it is a proof that you are born again —that you are a new creature in Christ Jesus.

But although you may be born again, it will require time to become a full-grown Christian. Justification is instantaneous; but sanctification is a life-work. We are to grow in wisdom. Peter says: "Grow in grace, and in the knowledge of our Lord and Saviour Jesus Christ" (2 Pet. iii. 18); and in the first chapter of his Second Epistle, "Add to your faith virtue; and to virtue knowledge; and to knowledge temperance; and to temperance patience; and to patience godliness; and to godliness brotherly kindness; and to brotherly kindness charity. For if these things be in you and abound they make you that ye shall neither be barren nor unfruitful in the knowledge of our Lord Jesus Christ." So that we are to add grace to grace. A tree may be perfect in its first year of growth; but it does not attain its maturity. So with the Christian: he may be a true child of God, but not a matured Christian. The eighth of Romans is very important, and we should be very familiar with it. In the fourteenth verse the apostle says:

"For as many as are led by the Spirit of God they are the sons of God." Just as the soldier is led by his captain, the pupil by his teacher, or the traveller by his guide; so the Holy Spirit will be the guide of every true child of God.

Then let me call your attention to another fact. All Paul's teaching in nearly every Epistle rings out the doctrine of assurance. He says in 2 Corinthians v. 1: "For we *know* that if our earthly house of this tabernacle were dissolved, we have a building of God, a house not made with hands, eternal in the heavens." He had a title to the mansions above, and he says—*I know it.* He was not living in uncertainty. He said: "I have a desire to depart and be with Christ" (Phil. i. 23); and if he had been uncertain he would not have said that. Then in Colossians iii. 4, he says: "When Christ, who is our life, shall appear, then shall ye also appear with Him in glory." I am told that Dr. Watts' tombstone bears this same passage of Scripture. There is no doubt there.

Then turn to Colossians i. 12: "Giving thanks unto the Father, which HATH made us meet to be partakers of the inheritance of the saints in light; who *hath* delivered us from the power of darkness, and *hath* translated us into the kingdom of His dear Son."

Three *haths* : "HATH made us meet;" "HATH delivered us;" and "HATH translated us." It does not say that He is going to make us meet; that He is going to deliver; that He is going to translate.

Then again in verse 14th: "In whom we have redemption through His blood, even the forgiveness of sins." We are either forgiven or we are not, we should not give ourselves any rest until we get into the kingdom of God; nor until we can each look up and say, "I know that if my earthly house of this tabernacle were dissolved, I have a building of God, a house not made with hands, eternal in the heavens" (2 Cor. v. 1).

Look at Romans viii. 32: "He that spared not His own Son, but delivered Him up for us all, how shall He not with Him also freely give us all things?" If He gave us His Son, will He not give us the certainty that He is ours. I have heard this illustration. There was a man who owed $10,-000, and would have been made a bankrupt, but a friend came forward and paid the sum. It was found afterwards that he owed a few dollars more; but he did not for a moment entertain a doubt that, as his friend had paid the larger amount, he would also pay the smaller. And we have high warrant for saying that if God has given us His Son He will with Him also freely give us all things; and if we want to realize our salvation beyond controversy He will not leave us in darkness.

Again in the 33d verse: "Who shall lay anything to the charge of God's elect? It is God that justifieth. Who is he that condemneth? It is Christ that died, yea rather, that is risen again, who is even at the right hand of God, who also maketh intercession for us. Who shall separate us from the love of Christ? shall tribulation, or distress, or persecution, or famine, or nakedness, or peril, or sword? As it is written, For Thy sake we are killed all the day long; we are accounted as sheep for the slaughter. Nay, in all these things we are more than conquerors through Him that loved us. For I am persuaded that neither death, nor life, nor angels, nor principalities, nor powers, nor things present, nor things to come, nor height, nor depth, nor any other creature, shall be able to separate us from the love of God, which is in Christ Jesus our Lord."

That has the right ring in it. There is Assurance for you. "I KNOW." Do you think that the God who has justified me will condemn me? That is quite an absurdity. God is going to save us so that neither men, angels, nor devils, can bring any charge against us or Him. He will have the work complete.

Job lived in a darker day than we do; but we read in Job xix. 25: "I *know* that my Redeemer liveth, and that He shall stand in the latter day upon the earth."

The same confidence breathes through Paul's last words to Timothy: "For the which cause I also suffer these things: nevertheless I am not ashamed; for I *know* whom I have believed, and am persuaded that He is able to keep that which I have committed unto Him against that day." It is not a matter of doubt, but of knowledge. "I know." "I am persuaded." The word "Hope," is not used in the Scripture to express doubt. It is used in regard to the second coming of Christ, or to the resurrection of the body. We do not say that we "hope" we are Christians. I do not say that I "hope" I am an American, or that I "hope" I am a married man. These are settled things. I may say that I "hope" to go back to my home, or I hope to attend such a meeting. I do not say that I "hope" to come to this country, for I am here. And so, if we are born of God we know it; and He will not leave us in darkness if we search the Scriptures.

Christ taught this doctrine to His seventy disciples when they returned elated with their success, saying, "Lord, even the devils are subject unto us through Thy name." The Lord seemed to check them, and said that He would give them something to rejoice in. "Notwithstanding in this rejoice not, that the spirits are subject unto you; but rather rejoice because your names are written in heaven." (Luke x. 20.)

It is the privilege of every one of us to know, beyond a a doubt, that our salvation is sure. Then we can work for others. But if we are doubtful of our own salvation, we are not fit for the service of God.

Another passage is John v. 24: "Verily, verily I say unto you: He that heareth my word, and believeth on Him that sent Me, hath everlasting life, and shall not come into '*judg-*

ment'" (the new translation has it so), "but is passed from death unto life."

Some people say that you never can tell till you are before the great white throne of Judgment whether you are saved or not. Why, my dear friend, if your life is hid with Christ in God, you are not coming into judgment for your sins. We may come into judgment for reward. This is clearly taught where the lord reckoned with the servant to whom five talents had been given, and who brought other five talents saying, "Lord, thou deliveredst unto me five talents; behold, I have gained beside them five talents more. His lord said unto him, Well done, thou good and faithful servant: thou hast been faithful over a few things; I will make thee ruler over many things; enter thou into the joy of thy lord." (Matt. xxv. 20, 21.) We shall be judged for our stewardship. That is one thing; but salvation—eternal life—is another.

Will God demand payment twice of the debt which Christ has paid for us? If Christ bear my sins in His own body on the tree, am I to answer for them as well?

Isaiah tells us that, "He was wounded for our transgressions; He was bruised for our iniquities; the chastisement of our peace was upon Him: and with His stripes we are healed." In Romans iv. 25, we read: He "was delivered for our offences, and was raised again for our justification." Let us believe, and get the benefit of His finished work.

Then again in John x. 9: "I am the door: by Me if any man enter in he shall be saved, and shall go in and out, and find pasture." That is the promise. Then the 27th verse, "My sheep hear my voice; and I know them, and they follow Me. And I give unto them eternal life; and they shall never perish, neither shall any man pluck them out of my hand. My father which gave them is greater than all; and no man is able to pluck them out of my Father's hand." Think of that! The Father, the Son, and the Holy Ghost, are pledged to keep us. You see that it is not only the Father, not only the Son, but the three persons of the Triune God.

Now, a great many people want some token outside of God's word. That habit always brings doubt. If I made a promise to meet a man at a certain hour and place to-morrow. and he were to ask me for my watch as a token of my sincerity, it would be a slur on my truthfulness. We must not question what God has said: He has made statement after statement, and multiplied figure upon figure. Christ says: "I am the door; by Me if any man enter in he shall be saved." "I am the Good Shepherd, and know My sheep, and am known of Mine." "I am the light of the world; he that followeth Me shall not walk in darkness, but shall have the light of life." "I am the truth;" receive Me, and you will have the truth; for I am the embodiment of truth. Do you want to know the way? "I am the way:" follow Me, and I will lead you into the kingdom. Are you hungering after righteousnes? "I am the Bread of life:" if you eat of Me you shall never hunger. "I am the Water of life:" if you drink of this water it shall be within you "a well of water springing up unto everlasting life." "I am the resurrection and the life: he that believeth in Me, though he were dead, yet shall he live; and whosoever liveth and believeth in Me shall never die." (John xi. 25, 26.)

Let me remind you where our doubts come from. A good many of God's dear people never get beyond knowing themselves servants. He calls us "friends." If you go into a house you will soon see the difference between the servant and the son. The son walks at perfect liberty all over the house; he is at home. But the servant takes a subordinate place. What we want is to get beyond servants. We ought to realize our standing with God as sons and daughters. He will not "un-child" His children. God has not only adopted us, but we are His by birth: we have been born into His kingdom. My little boy was as much mine when he was a day old as now that he is fourteen. He was *my son;* although it did not appear what he would be when he attained manhood. He is mine; although he may have to undergo probation under tutors and governors. The children of God are not perfect; but we are perfectly His children.

Another origin of doubts is looking at ourselves. If you want to be wretched and miserable, filled with doubts from morning till night, look at yourselves. "Thou wilt keep him in perfect peace whose mind is stayed on Thee." (Isa. xxvi. 3.) Many of God's dear children are robbed of joy because they keep looking at themselves.

Some one has said: "There are three ways to look. If you want to be wretched, look within; if you wish to be distracted, look around; but if you would have peace, look up." Peter looked away from Christ, and he immediately began to sink. The Master said to him: "O thou of little faith! Wherefore didst thou doubt?" (Matt. xiv. 31.) He had God's eternal word, which was sure footing, and better than either marble, granite or iron; but the moment he took his eyes off Christ down he went. Those who look around cannot see how unstable and dishonoring is their walk. We want to look straight at the "Author and Finisher of our faith"

When I was a boy I could only make a straight track in the snow, by keeping my eyes fixed upon a tree or some object before me. The moment I took my eye off the mark set in front of me, I walked crooked. It is only when we look fixedly on Christ that we find perfect peace. After He rose from the dead He showed His disciples His hands and His feet. (Luke xxiv. 40.) That was the ground of their peace. If you want to scatter your doubts, look at the blood; and if you want to increase your doubts, look at yourself. You will get doubts enough for years by being occupied with yourself for a few days.

Then again: look at what He is, and at what He has done; not at what you are, and what you have done. That is the way to get peace and rest.

Abraham Lincoln issued a proclamation declaring the emancipation of three millions of slaves. On a certain day their chains were to fall off, and they were to be free. The proclamation was put up on the trees and fences wherever the Northern Army marched. A good many slaves could not read: but others read the proclamation, and most of them believed it; and on a certain day a glad shout went up, "We are free!" Some did not believe it, and stayed with their old masters; but it did not alter the fact that they were free. Christ, the Captain of our salvation, has proclaimed freedom to all who have faith in Him. Let us take Him at His word. Their feelings would not have made the slaves free. The power must come from the outside. Looking at ourselves will not make us free, but it is looking to Christ with the eye of faith.

Bishop Ryle has strikingly said: "Faith is the root, and Assurance the flower. Doubtless you can never have the flower without the root; but it is no less certain you may have the root, and not the flower.

"Faith is that poor trembling woman who came behind Jesus in the press, and touched the hem of His garment. (Mark v. 27.) Assurance is Stephen standing calmly in the midst of his murderers, and saying, 'I see the heavens opened, and the Son of Man standing on the right hand of God' (Acts vii. 56).

"Faith is the penitent thief, crying, 'Lord, remember me' (Luke xxiii. 42). Assurance is Job sitting in the dust, covered with sores, and saying, 'I know that my Redeemer liveth;'

'Though He slay me, yet will I trust in Him' (Job xix. 25; xiii. 15).

"Faith is Peter's drowning cry, as he began to sink, 'Lord, save me!' (Matt. xxiv. 30). Assurance is that same Peter declaring before the Council, in after-times, 'This is the stone which was set at nought of you builders, which is become the head of the corner: neither is there salvation in any other; for there is none other name under heaven given among men whereby we must be saved' (Acts iv. 11, 12).

"Faith is the anxious, trembling voice, 'Lord, I believe; help Thou mine unbelief!' (Mark ix. 24). Assurance is the confident challenge, 'Who shall lay anything to the charge of God's elect? Who is he that condemneth?' (Rom. viii. 33, 34).

Faith is Saul praying in the house of Judas at Damascus, sorrowful, blind, and alone. (Acts ix. 11.) Assurance is Paul, the aged prisoner, looking camly into the grave, and saying, 'I know whom I have believed.' 'There is a crown laid up for me' (2 Tim. i. 12; iv. 8).

"Faith is LIFE. How great the blessing! Who can tell the gulf between life and death? And yet life may be weak, sickly, unhealthy, painful, trying, anxious, worn, burdensome, joyless, smileless, to the very end.

"Assurance is *more than life.* It is health, strength, power, vigor, activity, energy, manliness, beauty."

A minister once pronounced the benediction in this way: "The heart of God to make us welcome; the blood of Christ to make us clean, and the Holy Spirit to make us certain." The security of the believer is the result of the operation of the Spirit of God.

Another writer says: "I have seen shrubs and trees grow out of the rocks, and overhang fearful precipices, roaring cataracts, and deep running waters; but they maintained their position, and threw out their foliage and branches as much as if they had been in the midst of a dense forest." It was their hold on the rock that made them secure; and the influences of nature that sustained their life. So believers are oftentimes exposed to the most horrible dangers in their journey to heaven; but, so long as they are "rooted and grounded" in the Rock of Ages, they are perfectly secure. Their hold of Him is their guarantee; and the blessings of His grace give them life and sustain them in life. And as the tree must die, or the rock fall, before a dissolution can be effected between *them*, so either the believer must lose his spiritual life, or the Rock must crumble, ere their union can be dissolved.

Speaking of the Lord Jesus, Isaiah says: "I will fasten Him as a nail in a sure place; and He shall be for a glorious throne to His Father's house: and they shall hang upon Him all the glory of His father's house, the offspring and the issue, all vessels of small quantity, from the vessels of cups, even to all the vessels of flagons" (xxii. 23, 24).

There is ONE NAIL, fastened in a sure place; and on it hang all the flagons and all the cups. "Oh," says one little cup, "I am so small and so black, suppose I were to drop!" "Oh," says a flagon, "there is no fear of you; but I am so heavy, so very weighty, suppose I were to drop!" And a little cup says, "Oh, if I were only like the gold cup there, I should never fear falling." But the gold cup answers, "It is not because I am a gold cup that I keep up; but because I hang upon the nail." If the nail gives way we all come down, gold cups, china cups, pewter cups, and all; but as long as the nail keeps up, all that hang on Him hang safely.

I once read these words on a tombstone: "Born, died, kept." Let us pray God to keep us in perfect peace, and assured of salvation.

CHAPTER VIII.

CHRIST ALL AND IN ALL.

(COLOSSIANS iii. 11.)

CHRIST is *all* to us that we make Him to be. I want to emphasize that word "ALL." Some men make Him to be "a root out of a dry ground," "without form or comeliness." He is nothing to them; they do not want Him. Some Christians have a very small Saviour, for they are not willing to receive Him fully, and let Him do great and mighty things for them. Others have a mighty Saviour, because they make Him to be great and mighty.

If we would know what Christ wants to be to us, we must first of all know Him as our Saviour from sin. When the angel came down from heaven to proclaim that He was to be born into the world, you remember he gave His name, "He shall be called JESUS,* for He shall save His people from their sins." HAVE WE BEEN DELIVERED FROM SIN? He did not come to save us *in* our sins, but *from* our sins. Now, there are three ways of knowing a man. Some men you know only by hearsay; others you merely know by having been once introduced to them, you know them very slightly; other again you know by having been acquainted with them for years, you know them intimately. So I believe there are three classes of people to-day in the Christian Church and out of it: those who know Christ only by reading or by hearsay, those who have a historical Christ; those who have a slight personal acquaintance with Him; and, those who thirst, as Paul did, to

*Saviour.

"know Him and the power of His resurrection." The more we know of Christ the more we shall love Him, and the better we shall serve Him.

Let us look at Him as He hangs upon the Cross, and see how He has put away sin. He was manifested that He might take away our sins; and if we really know Him we must first of all see Him as our Saviour from sin. You remember how the angels said to the shepherds on the plains of Bethlehem, "Behold, I bring you good tidings of great joy, which shall be to all people: for unto you is born this day, in the city of David, a Saviour, which is Christ the Lord." (Luke ii. 10, 11.) Then if you go clear back to Isaiah, seven hundred years before Christ's birth, you will find these words: "I, even I, am the Lord; and beside me there is no Saviour" (xliii. 11).

Again, in the First Epistle of John (iv. 14) we read: "We have seen, and do testify, that the Father sent the Son to be the Saviour of the world." All the heathen religions, we read, teach men to work their way up to God; but the religion of Jesus Christ is God coming down to men to save them, to lift them up out of the pit of sin. In Luke xix. 10, we read that Christ Himself told the people what He had come for: "The Son of Man is come to seek and to save that which was lost." So we start from the Cross, not from the cradle. Christ has opened up a new and living way to the Father; He has taken all the stumbling-blocks out of the way, so that every man who accepts of Christ as his Saviour can have salvation.

But Christ is not only a Saviour. I might save a man from drowning and rescue him from an untimely grave; but I might probably not be able to do any more for him. Christ is something more than a Saviour. When the children of Israel were placed behind the blood, that blood was their salvation; but they would still have heard the crack of the slave-driver's whip if they had not been delivered from the Egyptian yoke of bondage: then it was that God delivered them from the hand of the king of Egypt. I have little sympathy with the idea that God comes down to save us, and then leaves us in prison, the slaves of our besetting sins. No; He has come to deliver us, and to give us victory over our evil tempers, our passions, and our lusts. Are you a professed Christian but one who is a slave to some besetting sin? If you want to get victory over that temper or that lust, go on to know Christ more intimately. He brings deliverance for the past, the present, and the future. "Who delivered; who doth deliver; who will yet deliver." (2 Cor. i. 10.)

How often, like the children of Israel when they came to the Red Sea, have we become discouraged because everything looked dark before us, behind us, and around us, and we knew not which way to turn. Like Peter we have said, "To whom shall we go?" But God has appeared for our deliverance. He has brought us through the Red Sea right out into the wilderness, and opened up the way into the Promised Land. But Christ is not only our Deliverer; He is our Redeemer. That is something more than being our Saviour. He has brought us back. "Ye have sold yourselves for nought; and ye shall be redeemed without money." (Isaiah lii. 3.) We were not redeemed with corruptible things, as silver and gold." (1 Peter i. 18.) If gold could have redeemed us, could He not have created ten thousand worlds full of gold?

When God had redeemed the children of Israel from the bondage of Egypt, and brought them through the Red Sea, they struck out for the wilderness; and then God became to them their Way. I am so thankful the Lord has not left us in darkness as to the right way. There is no living man who has been groping in the darkness but may know the way. "I am the Way," says Christ. If we follow Christ we shall be in the right way, and have the right doctrine. Who could lead the children of Israel through the wilderness like the Almighty God Himself? He knew the pitfalls and dangers of the way, and guided the people through all their wilderness journey right into the promised land. It is true that if it had not been for their accursed unbelief they might have crossed into the land at Kadesh Barnea, and taken possession of it, but they desired something besides God's word; so they were turned back, and had to wander in the desert for forty years. I believe there are thousands of God's children wandering in the wilderness still. The Lord has delivered them from the hand of the Egyptian, and would at once take them through the wilderness right into the Promised Land, if they were only willing to follow Christ. Christ has been down here, and has made the rough places smooth, and the dark places light, and the crooked places straight. If we will only be led by Him, and will follow Him, all will be peace, and joy, and rest.

In the frontier, when a man goes out hunting he takes a hatchet with him, and cuts off pieces from the bark of the trees as he goes along through the forest: this is called "blazing the way." He does it that he may know the way back, as there is no pathway through these thick forests. Christ has come down to this earth; He has "blazed the Way:" and now that He has gone up on high, if we will but follow him, we shall be kept in the right path. I will tell you how you may know if you are following Christ or not. If some one has slandered you, or misjudged you, do you treat them as your master would have done? If you do not bear these things in a loving and forgiving spirit, all the churches and ministers in the world cannot make you right. "If any man have not the Spirit of Christ, he is none of His." (Romans viii. 9.) "If any man be in Christ Jesus he is a new creature: old things are passed away; behold, all things are become new." (2 Cor. v. 17.)

Christ is not only our way· He is the Light upon the way. He says, "I am the Light of the world." (John viii. 12; ix. 5; xii. 46.) He goes on to say, "He that followeth Me shall not walk in darkness, but shall have the light of life." It is impossible for any man or woman who is following Christ to walk in darkness. If your soul is in the darkness, groping around in the fog and mist of earth, let me tell you it is because you have got away from the true light. There is nothing but light that will dispel darkness. So let those who are walking in spiritual darkness admit Christ into their hearts: He is the Light. I call to mind a picture of which I used at one time to think a good deal; but now I have come to look more closely, I would not put it up in my house except I turned the face to the wall. It represents Christ as standing at a door, knocking, and having a big lantern in His hand. Why, you might as well hang up a lantern to the sun as put one into Christ's hand. He is the Sun of Righteousness; and it is our privilege to walk in the light of an unclouded sun.

Many people are hunting after light, and peace, and joy. We are nowhere told to seek after these things. If we admit Christ into our hearts these will all come of themselves. I remember, when a boy, I used to try in vain to catch my shadow. One day I was walking with my face to the sun; and as I happened to look around I saw that my shadow was following me. The faster I went the faster my shadow followed; I could not get away from it. So when our faces are directed to the Sun of Righteousness, the peace and joy are sure to come. A man said to me some time ago, "Moody, how do you feel?" It was so long since I had thought about my feelings I had to stop and consider awhile, in order to find out. Some Christians are all the time thinking about their feelings; and because they do not feel just right they think their joy is all gone. If we keep our faces towards Christ, and are occupied with Him, we shall be lifted out of the darkness and the trouble that may have gathered round our path.

I remember being in a meeting after the war of the great rebellion broke out. The war had been going on for about six months. The army of the North had been defeated at Bull Run, in fact, we had nothing but defeat, and it looked as though the republic was going to pieces. So we were much cast down and discouraged. At this meeting every speaker for awhile seemed as if he had hung his harp upon the willow; and it was one of the gloomiest meetings I ever attended. Finally an old man with beautiful white hair got up to speak, and his face literally shone. "Young men," he said "you do not talk like sons of the King. Though it is dark just here, remember it is light somewhere else." Then he went on to say that if it were dark all over the world, it was light up around the Throne.

He told us he had come from the east, where a friend had described to him how he had been up a mountain to spend the night and see the sun rise. As the party were climbing up the mountain, and before they had reached the summit, a storm came on. This friend said to the guide, "I will give this up; take me back." The guide smiled, and replied, "I think we shall get above the storm soon." On they went; and it was not long before they got up to where it was as calm as any summer evening. Down in the valley a terrible storm raged; they could hear the thunder rolling, and see the lightning's flash; but all was serene on the mountain top. "And so, my young friends," continued the old man, "though all is dark around you, come a little higher and the darkness will flee away." Often when I have been inclined to get discouraged, I have thought of what he said. Now if you are down in the valley amidst the thick fog and the darkness, get a little higher; get nearer to Christ, and know more of Him.

You remember the Bible says, that when Christ expired on the cross, the light of the world was put out. God sent His Son to be the light of the world; but men did not love the light because it reproved them of their sins. When they were about to put out this light, what did Christ say to His disciples? "Ye shall be witnesses unto Me." (Acts i. 8.) He has gone up yonder to intercede for us; but He wants us to shine for Him down here. "Ye are the light of the world." (Matt. v. 14.) So our work is to shine; not to blow our own trumpet so that people may look at us. What we want to do is to show forth Christ. If we have any light at all it is borrowed light. Some one said to a young Christian: "Converted! it is all moonshine!" Said he: "I thank you for the illustration; the moon borrows its light from the sun; and we borrow ours from the Sun of Righteousness." If we are Christ's, we are here to shine for Him: by and by he will call us home to our reward.

I remember hearing of a blind man who sat by the wayside with a lantern near him. When he was asked what he had a lantern for, as he could not see the light, he said it was that people should not stumble over him. I believe more people stumble over the inconsistencies of professed Christians than from any other cause. What is doing more harm to the cause of Christ than all the scepticism in the world is this cold, dead formalism, this conformity to the world, this professing what we do not possess. The eyes of the world are upon us. I think it was George Fox who said every Quaker ought to light up the country for ten miles around him. If we were all brightly shining for the Master, those about us would soon be reached, and there would be a shout of praise going to heaven.

People say: "I want to know what is the truth." Listen: "I AM THE TRUTH," says Christ. (John xiv. 5.) If you want to know what the truth is, get acquainted with Christ. People also complain that they have not life. Many are trying to give themselves spiritual life. You may galvanize yourselves and put electricity into yourselves, so to speak; but the effect will not last very long. Christ alone is the author of life. If you would have real spiritual life, get to know Christ. Many try to stir up spiritual life by going to meetings. That may be well enough; but it will be of no use, unless they get into contact with the living Christ. Then their spiritual life will not be a spasmodic thing, but will be perpetual; flowing on and on, and bringing forth fruit to God.

Then Christ is our KEEPER. A great many young disciples are afraid they will not hold out. "He that keepeth Israel shall neither slumber nor sleep." (Psalm cxxi. 4.) It is the work of Christ to keep us; and if He keeps us there will be no danger of our falling. I suppose if Queen Victoria had to take care of the Crown of England, some thief might attempt to get access to it; but it is put away in the Tower of London, and guarded night and day by soldiers. The whole English army would, if necessary, be called out to protect it. And we have no strength in ourselves. We are no match for Satan; he has had six thousand years' experience. But then we remember that the One who neither slumbers nor sleeps is our keeper. In Isaiah xli. 10, we read, "Fear thou not, for I am with thee; be not dismayed, for I am thy God; I will strengthen thee; yea, I will help thee; yea, I will uphold thee with the right hand of My righteousness." In Jude also, verse 24, we are told that He is "able to keep us from falling." "We have an Advocate with the Father, Jesus Christ the righteous." (1 John ii. 1.)

But Christ is something more. He is our SHEPHERD. It is the work of the shepherd to care for the sheep, to feed them and protect them. "I am the Good Shepherd;" "My sheep hear My voice." "I lay down My life for the sheep." In that wonderful tenth chapter of John, Christ uses the personal pronoun no less than twenty-eight times, in declaring what He is and what He will do. In verse 28 He says, "They shall never perish; neither shall any [*man*] pluck them out of My hand." But notice the word "man" is in italics. See how the verse really reads: "Neither shall ANY pluck them out of My hand"—no devil or man shall be able to do it. In another place the Scripture declares, "Your life is hid with Christ in God." (Col. iii. 3.) How safe and how secure!

Christ says, "My sheep hear My voice . . . and they follow Me." (John x. 27.) A gentleman in the East heard of a shepherd who could call all his sheep to him by name. He went and asked if this was true. The shepherd took him to the pasture where they were, and called one of them by some name. One sheep looked up and answered the call, while the others went on feeding and paid no attention. In the same way he called about a dozen of the sheep around him. The stranger said, "How do you know one from the other? They all look perfectly alike." "Well," said he, "you see that sheep toes in a little; that other one has a squint; one has a little piece of wool off; another has a black spot; and another has a piece out of its ear." The man knew all his sheep by their failings, for he had not a perfect one in the whole flock. I suppose our Shepherd knows us in the same way.

An Eastern shepherd was once telling a gentleman that his sheep knew his voice, and that no stranger could deceive them. The gentleman thought he would like to put the statement to the test. So he put on the shepherd's frock and turban, and took his staff and went to the flock. He disguised his voice, and tried to speak as much like the shepherd as he could; but he could not get a single sheep in the flock to follow him. He asked the shepherd if his sheep never followed a stranger. He was obliged to admit that if a sheep got sickly it would follow any one. So it is with a good many professed Christians; when they get sickly and weak in the faith, they will follow any teacher that comes along; but when the soul is in health, a man will not be carried away by errors and heresies. He will know whether the "voice" speaks the truth or not. He can soon tell that, if he is really in communion with God. When God sends a true messenger his words will find a ready response in the Christian heart.

Christ is a tender Shepherd. You may some time think He has not been a very tender Shepherd to you; you are passing under the rod. It it written, "Whom the Lord loveth He chasteneth, and scourgeth every son whom He receiveth." (Heb. xii. 6.) That you are passing under the rod is no proof that Christ does not love you. A friend of mine lost all his children. No man could ever have loved his family more; but the scarlet fever took one by one away; and so the whole four or five, one after another, died. The poor stricken parents went over to great Britain, and wandered from one place to another, there and on the continent. At length they found their way to Syria. One day they saw an Eastern shepherd come down to a stream, and call his flock to cross. The sheep came down to the brink, and looked at the water; but they seemed to shrink from it, and he could not get them to respond to his call. He then took a little lamb, put it under one arm; he took another lamb and put it under the other arm, and thus passed into the stream. The old sheep no longer stood looking at the water: they plunged in after the shepherd; and in a few minutes the whole flock was on the other side; and he led them away to newer and fresher pastures. The bereaved father and mother, as they looked on the scene, felt that it taught them a lesson. They no longer murmured because the Great Shepherd had taken their lambs one by one into yonder world; and they began to look up and look forward to the time when they would follow the loved ones they had lost. If you have loved ones gone before, remember that your Shepherd is calling you to "set your affection on things above." (Col. iii. 2.) Let us be faithful to Him, and follow Him, while we remain in this world. And if you have not taken Him for your Shepherd, do so this very day.

Christ is not only all these things that I have mentioned: He is also our Mediator, our Sanctifier, our Justifier; in fact, it would take volumes to tell what He desires to be to every individual soul. While looking through some papers I once read this wonderful description of Christ. I do not know where it originally came from; but it was so fresh to my soul that I should like to give it to you:—

"Christ is our Way; we walk in Him. He is our Truth; we embrace Him. He is our Life; we live in Him. He is our Lord; we choose Him to rule over us. He is our Master; we serve Him. He is our Teacher, instructing us in the way of salvation. He is our Prophet, pointing out the future. He is our Priest, having atoned for us. He is our Advocate, ever living to make intercession for us. He is our Saviour, saving to the uttermost. He is our Root; we grow from Him. He is our Bread; we feed upon Him. He is our Shepherd, leading us into green pastures. He is our true Vine; we abide in Him. He is the Water of Life; we slake our thirst from Him. He is the fairest among ten thousand: we admire Him above all others. He is 'the brightness of the Father's glory, and the express image of His person;' we strive to reflect His likeness. He is the upholder of all things; we rest upon Him. He is our wisdom; we are guided by Him. He is our Righteousness; we cast all our imperfections upon Him. He is our Sanctification; we draw all our power for holy life from Him. He is our Redemption, redeeming us from all iniquity. He is our Healer, curing all our diseases. He is our Friend, relieving us in all our necessities. He is our Brother, cheering us in our difficulties."

Here is another beautiful extract: it is from Gotthold:

"For my part, my soul is like a hungry and thirsty child; and I need His love and consolation for my refreshment. I am a wandering and lost sheep; and I need Him as a good and faithful shepherd. My soul is like a frightened dove pursued by the hawk; and I need His wounds for a refuge. I am a feeble vine; and I need His cross to lay hold of, and to wind myself about. I am a sinner; and I need His righteousness. I am naked and bare; and I need His holiness and innocence for a covering. I am ignorant; and I need His teaching: simple and foolish; and I need the guidance of His Holy Spirit. In no situation, and at no time, can I do without Him. Do I pray? He must prompt, and intercede for me. Am I arraigned by Satan at the Divine tribunal? He must be my Advocate. Am I in affliction? He must be my Helper. Am I persecuted by the world? He must defend me, When I am forsaken, He must be my Support; when I am dying, my life: when mouldering in the grave, my Resurrection. Well, then, I will rather part with all the world, and all that it contains, than with Thee, my Saviour. And, God be thanked! I know that Thou, too, art neither able nor willing to do without me. Thou art rich; and I am poor. Thou hast abundance; and I am needy. Thou hast righteousness; and I sins. Thou hast wine and oil; and I wounds. Thou hast cordials and refreshments; and I hunger and thirst.

Use me then, my Saviour, for whatever purpose, and in whatever way, Thou mayest require. Here is my poor heart, an empty vessel; fill it with Thy grace. Here is my sinful and troubled soul; quicken and refresh it with Thy love. Take my heart for Thine abode; my mouth to spread the glory of Thy name; my love and all my powers, for the advancement of Thy believing people; and never suffer the steadfastness and confidence of my faith to abate—that so at all times I may be enabled from the heart to say, 'Jesus needs me, and I Him; and so we suit each other.'"

CHAPTER IX.

BACKSLIDING.

"I will heal their backsliding; I will love them freely: for Mine anger is turned away.'—Hosea xiv. 4.

There are two kinds of backsliders. Some have never been converted: they have gone through the form of joining a Christian community and claim to be backsliders; but they never have, if I may use the expression, "slid forward." They may talk of back-sliding; but they have never really been born again. They need to be treated differently from real back-sliders—those who have been born of the incorruptible seed, but who have turned aside. We want to bring the latter back the same road by which they left their first love.

Turn to Psalm lxxxv. 5. There you read: "Wilt Thou be angry with us for ever? wilt Thou draw out Thine anger to all generations? wilt Thou not revive us again: that Thy people may rejoice in Thee? Show us Thy mercy, O Lord; and grant us Thy salvation." Now look again: "*I will hear what God the Lord will speak:* for He will speak peace unto His people, and to His saints; but let them not turn again to folly "(*verse* 8).

There is nothing that will do back-sliders so much good as to come in contact with the Word of God; and for them the Old Testament is as full of help as the New. The book of Jeremiah has some wonderful passages for wanderers. What we want to do is to get back-sliders to hear what God the Lord will say.

Look for a moment at Jeremiah vi. 10. "To whom shall I speak, and give warning, that they may hear? behold, their ear is uncircumcised, and they cannot hearken: behold, the word of the Lord is unto them a reproach; they have no delight in it." That is the condition of back-sliders. They have no delight whatever in the word of God. But we want to bring them back, and let God get their ear. Read from the 14th verse: "They have healed also the hurt of the daughter of My people slightly, saying, Peace, peace; when there is no peace. Were they ashamed when they had committed abomination? nay, they were not at all ashamed, neither could they blush: therefore they shall fall among them that fall: at the time that I visit them they shall be cast down, saith the Lord. Thus saith the Lord, Stand ye in the ways, and see, and ask for the old paths, where is the good way, and walk therein; and ye shall find rest for your souls. But they said, We will not walk therein. Also I set watchmen over you, saying, Hearken to the sound of the trumpet. But they said, We will not hearken."

That was the condition of the Jews when they had backslidden. They had turned away from the old paths. And that is the condition of backsliders. They have got away from the good old book. Adam and Eve fell by not hearkening to the word of God. They did not believe God's word; but they believed the tempter. That is the way backsliders fall—by turning away from the word of God.

In Jeremiah ii. we find God pleading with them as a father would plead with a son. "Thus saith the Lord, What iniquity have your fathers found in Me, that they are gone from Me, and have walked after vanity, and are become vain? . . . Wherefore I will yet plead with you, saith the Lord; and with your children's children will I plead . . . For my people have committed two evils: they have forsaken Me, the Fountain of living waters; and hewed them out cisterns, broken cisterns, that can hold no water."

Now there is one thing to which we wish to call the attention of backsliders; and that is, that the Lord never forsook them; but that they forsook Him! The Lord never left them; but they left Him! And this, too, without any cause! He says: "What iniquity have your fathers found in Me, that they are gone far from Me?" Is not God the same to-day as when you came to Him first? Has God changed? Men are apt to think that God has changed; but the fault is with them. Backslider, I would ask you, "What iniquity is there in God, that you have left Him and gone far from Him?" You have, He says, hewed out to yourselves broken cisterns that hold no water. The world cannot satisfy the new nature. No earthly well can satisfy the soul that has become a partaker of the heavenly nature. Honor, wealth and the pleasures of this world, will not satisfy those who, having tasted the water of life, have gone astray, seeking refreshment at the world's fountains. Earthly wells will get dry. They cannot quench spiritual thirst.

Again: in the 32d verse. "Can a maid forget her ornaments, or a bride her attire? yet My yeople have forgotten Me, days without number. That is the charge which God brings against the backslider. They "have forgotten Me, days without number."

I have often startled young ladies when I have said to them, "My friend, you think more of your ear-rings than of the Lord." The reply has been, "No, I do not." But when I have asked, "Would you not be troubled if you lost one; and would you not set about seeking for it?" the answer has been, "Well, yes, I think I should." But though they had turned from the Lord, it did not give them any trouble; nor did they seek after Him that they might find Him.

How many once in fellowship and in daily communion with the Lord now think more of their dresses and ornaments than of their precious souls! Love does not like to be forgotten. Mothers would have broken hearts if their children left them and never wrote a word or sent any memento of their affection; and God pleads over backsliders as a parent over loved ones who have gone astray. He tries to woo them back: He asks: "What have I done that you should have forsaken Me?"

The most tender and loving words to be found in the whole of the Bible are from Jehovah to those who have left Him without a cause. Jer. ii. 19.

Hear how He argues with such: (Jer. xi. 19.) "Thine own wickedness shall correct thee, and thy backslidings shall reprove thee; know, therefore, and see, that it is an evil thing and bitter, that thou hast forsaken the Lord thy God, and that My fear is not in thee, saith the Lord God of hosts."

I do not exaggerate when I say that I have seen hundreds of backsliders come back; and I have asked them if they have not found it an evil and a bitter thing to leave the Lord. You cannot find a real backslider, who has known the Lord, but will admit that it is an evil and a bitter thing to turn away from Him; and I do not know of any one verse more used to bring back wanderers than that very one. May it bring you back if you have wandered into the far country.

Look at Lot. Did not he find it an evil and a bitter thing? He was twenty years in Sodom, and never made a convert. He got on well in the sight of the world. Men would have told you that he was one of the most influential and worthy men in all Sodom. But alas! alas! he ruined his family. And it is a pitiful sight to see that old backslider going through the streets of Sodom at midnight, after he has warned his children, and they have turned a deaf ear.

I have never known a man and his wife backslide, without its proving utter ruin to their children. They will make a mockery of religion and will deride their parents: "Thine own wickedness shall correct thee; and thy backsliding shall reprove thee!" Did not David find it so? Mark him, crying, "O my son Absalom, my son, my son Absalom! would God I had died for thee; O Absalom, my son, my son!" I think it was the ruin, rather than the death of his son that caused this anguish.

I remember being engaged in conversation some years ago, till past midnight, with an old man. He had been for years wandering on the barren mountains of sin. That night he wanted to get back. We prayed, and prayed, and prayed, till light broke in upon him; and he went away rejoicing. The next night he sat in front of me when I was preaching, and I think that I never saw any one look so sad and wretched in all my life. He followed me into the enquiry-room. "What is the trouble?" I asked. "Is your eye off the Saviour? Have your doubts come back?" "No; it is not that," he said. "I did not go to business, but spent all this day in visiting my children. They are all married and in this city. I went from house to house, but there was not one but mocked me. It is the darkest day of my life. I have awoke up to what I have done. I have taken my children into the world; and now I cannot get them out." The Lord had restored unto him the joy of His salvation; yet there was the bitter consequence of his transgression. You can run through your experience; and you can find just such instances repeated again and again. Many who came to your city years ago serving God, in their prosperity have forgotten Him: and where are their sons and daughters? Show me the father and mother who have deserted the Lord and gone back to the beggarly elements of the world; and I am mistaken if their children are not on the high road to ruin.

As we desire to be faithful we warn these backsliders. It is a sign of love to warn of danger. We may be looked upon as enemies for a while; but the truest friends are those who lift up the voice of warning. Israel had no truer friend than Moses. In Jeremiah God gave His people a weeping prophet to bring them back to Him; but they cast off God. They forgot the God who brought them out of Egypt, and who led them through the desert into the promised land. In their prosperity they forget Him and turned away. The Lord had told them what would happen. (Deut. xxviii.) And see what did happen. The king who make light of the word of God was taken captive by Nebuchadnezzar, and his children brought up in front of him and every one slain: his eyes were put out of his head; and he was bound in fetters of brass and cast into a dungeon in Babylon. (2 Kings xxv. 7.) That is the way he reaped what he had sown. Surely it is an evil and a bitter thing to backslide, but the Lord would win you back with the message of His Work.

In Jeremiah viii. 5, we read: "Why then is this people of Jerusalem slidden by a perpetual backsliding? They hold fast deceit; *They refuse to return.*" That is what the Lord brings against them. "THEY REFUSE TO RETURN." "I hearkened and heard: but they spake not aright: no man repented him of his wickedness, saying, What have I done? Every one turned to his course, as the horse rusheth into the battle. Yea, the stork in the heaven knoweth her appointed times; and the turtle and the crane and the swallow observe the time of their coming; but My people know not the judgment of the Lord."

Now look: "I hearkened and heard; but they spake not aright." No family altar! No reading the Bible! No closet devotion! God stoops to hear; but His people have turned away! If there be a penitent backslider, one who is anxious for pardon and restoration, you will find no words more tender than are to be found in Jeremiah iii. 12: "Go, and proclaim these words toward the north, and say, Return, thou backsliding Israel, saith the Lord; and I will not cause Mine anger to fall upon you: for I am merciful, saith the Lord, and I will not keep anger forever." Now notice: "Only acknowledge thine iniquity, that thou hast transgressed against the Lord thy God, and hast scattered thy ways to the stranger under every green tree, and ye have not obeyed My voice, saith the Lord. Turn, O backsliding children, saith the Lord; for I am married unto you"—think of God coming and saying, "*I am married unto you!*—and I will take you one of a city, and two of a family, and I will bring you to Zion."

"Only acknowledge thine iniquity." How many times have I held that passage up to a backslider! "Acknowledge" it; and God says I will forgive you. I remember a man asking, "Who said that? Is that there?" And I held up to him the passage, "Only acknowledge thine iniquity;" and the man went down on his knees, and cried, "My God, I have sinned"; and the Lord restored him there and then. If you have wandered, He wants you to come back.

He says in another place, "O Ephraim, what shall I do unto thee? O Judah, what shall I do unto thee? for your goodness is as a morning cloud, and as the early dew it goeth away" (Hosea vi. 4). His compassion and His love is wonderful!

In Jeremiah iii. 22; "Return, ye backsliding children, and I will heal your backslidings. Behold, we come unto Thee; Thou art the Lord our God." He just puts words into the mouth of the backslider. Only come; and, if you will come, He will receive you graciously and love you freely.

In Hosea xiv. 1, 2, 4: "O Israel, return unto the Lord thy God; for thou hast fallen by thine iniquity. Take with you words, and turn to the Lord (He puts words into your mouth):

say unto Him, Take away all iniquity, and receive us graciously: so will we render the calves of our lips . . . I will heal their backsliding, I will love them freely, for Mine anger is turned away from him." Just observe that, Turn! *Turn!!* TURN!!! rings all through these passages.

Now, if you have wandered, remember that you left Him, and not He you. You have to get out of the backslider's pit just in the same way you got in. And if you take the same road as when you left the Master you will find Him now, just where you are.

If we were to treat Christ as any earthly friend we should never leave Him; and there would never be a backslider. If I were in a town for a single week I should not think of going away without shaking hands with the friends I had made, and saying "Good bye" to them. I should be justly blamed if I took the train and left without saying a word to any one. The cry would be, "What's the matter?" But did you ever hear of a backslider bidding the Lord Jesus Christ "Good bye"; going into his closet and saying "Lord Jesus, I have known Thee ten, twenty, or thirty years: but I am tired of Thy service; Thy yoke is not easy, nor Thy burden light; so I am going back to the world, to the flesh-pots of Egypt. Good bye, Lord Jesus! Farewell"? Did you ever hear that? No; you never did, and you never will. I tell you, if you get into the closet and shut out the world and hold communion with the Master you cannot leave Him. The language of your heart will be, "To whom shall we go," but unto Thee? "Thou hast the words of eternal life" (John vi. 68). You could not go back to the world if you treated Him in that way. But you left Him and ran away. You have forgotten Him days without number. Come back to-day; just as you are! Make up your mind that you will not rest until God has restored unto you the joy of His salvation.

A gentleman in Cornwall once met a Christian in the street whom he knew to be a backslider. He went up to him, and said: "Tell me, is there not some estrangement between you and the Lord Jesus?" The man hung his head, and said, "Yes." "Well," said the gentleman, "what has He done to you?" The answer to which was a flood of tears.

In Revelation ii. 4, 5, we read: "Nevertheless I have somewhat against thee, because thou hast left the first love. Remember therefore from whence thou art fallen; and repent, and do the first works: or else I will come unto thee quickly, and will remove thy candlestick out of his place, except thou repent." I want to guard you against a mistake which some people make with regard to "doing the first works." Many think that they are to have the same experience over again. That has kept thousands for months without peace; because they have been waiting for a renewal of their first experience. You will never have the same experience as when you first came to the Lord. God never repeats himself. No two people of all earth's millions look alike or think alike. You may say that you cannot tell two people apart; but when you get well acquainted with them you can very quickly distinguish differences. So, no one person will have the same experience a second time. If God will restore His joy to your soul let Him do it in His way. Do not mark out a way for God to bless you. Do not expect the same experience that you had two or twenty years ago. You will have a fresh experience, and God will deal with you in His own way. If you confess your sins and tell Him that you have wandered from the path of His commandments He will restore unto you the joy of His salvation.

I want to call your attention to the manner in which Peter fell; and I think that nearly all fall pretty much in the same way. I want to lift up a warning note to those who have not fallen. "Let him that thinketh he standeth, take heed lest he fall" (1 Cor. x. 12). Twenty-five years ago—and for the first five years after I was converted—I used to think that if I were able to stand for twenty years I need fear no fall. But the nearer you get to the Cross the fiercer the battle. Satan aims high. He went amongst the twelve; and singled out the Treasurer—Judas Iscariot, and the Chief Apostle—Peter. Most men who have fallen have done so on the strongest side of their character. I am told that the only side upon which Edinburgh Castle was successfully assailed was where the rocks were steepest, and where the garrison thought themselves secure. If any man thinks that he is strong enough to resist the devil at any one point he needs special watch there, for the tempter comes that way.

Abraham stands, as it were, at the head of the family of faith; and the children of faith may be said to trace their descent to Abraham: and yet down in Egypt he denied his wife. (Gen. xii.) Moses was noted for his meekness; and yet he was kept out of the promised land because of one hasty act and speech, when he was told by the Lord to speak to the rock so that the congregation and their beasts should have water to drink. "Hear now, ye rebels; must we fetch you water out of this rock?" (Num. xx. 10).

Elijah was remarkable for his boldness: and yet he went off a day's journey into the wilderness like a coward and hid himself under a juniper tree, requesting for himself that he might die, because of a message he received from a woman. (1 Kings xix.) Let us be careful. No matter who the man is —he may be in the pulpit—but if he gets self-conceited he will be sure to fall. We who are followers of Christ need constantly to pray to be made humble, and kept humble. God made Moses' face so to shine that other men could see it; but Moses himself wist not that his face shone, and the more holy in heart a man is the more manifest to the outer world will be his daily life and conversation. Some people talk of how humble they are; but if they have true humility there will be no necessity for them to publish it. It is not needful. A lighthouse does not have a drum beaten or a trumpet blown in order to proclaim the proximity of a lighthouse: it is its own witness. And so if we have the true light in us it will show itself. It is not those who make the most noise who have the most piety. There is a brook, or a little "burn" as the Scotch call it, not far from where I live; and after a heavy rain you can hear the rush of its waters a long way off: but let there come a few days of pleasant weather, and the brook becomes almost silent. But there is a river near my house, the flow of which I never heard in my life, as it pours on in its deep and majestic course the year round. We should have so much of the love of God within us that its presence shall be evident without our loud proclamation of the fact.

The first step in Peter's downfall was his self-confidence. The Lord warned him. The Lord said: "Simon, Simon, behold, Satan hath desired to have you, that he may sift you as wheat: but I have prayed for thee, that thy faith fail not" (Luke xxii. 31, 32). But Peter said: "I am ready to go with Thee, both into prison and to death." "Though all shall be offended because of Thee, yet will I never be offended." (Matt. xxvi. 23.) "James and John, and the others, may leave You; but You can count on me!" But the Lord warned him: "I tell thee, Peter, the cock shall not crow this day, before that thou shalt thrice deny that thou knowest Me." (Luke xxii. 24.)

Though the Lord rebuked him, Peter said he was ready to follow Him to death. That boasting is too often a forerunner of downfall. Let us walk humbly and softly. We have a great tempter; and, in an unguarded hour, we may stumble and fall and bring a scandal on Christ.

The next step in Peter's downfall was that he went to sleep. If Satan can rock the Church to sleep he does his work through God's own people. Instead of Peter watching one short hour in Gethsemane, he fell asleep, and the Lord asked him, "What, could ye not watch with Me one hour?" (Matt. xxvi. 40.) The next thing was that he fought in the energy of the flesh. The Lord rebuked him again and said, "They that take the sword shall perish with the sword." (Matt. xxvi. 52.) Jesus had to undo what Peter had done. The next thing, he "followed afar off." Step by step he gets away. It is a sad thing when a child of God follows afar off. When you see him associating with worldly friends, and throwing his influence on the wrong side, he is following afar off; and it will not be long before disgrace will be brought upon the old family name, and Jesus Christ will be wounded in the house of his friends. The man, by his example, will cause others to stumble and fall.

The next thing—Peter is familiar and friendly with the enemies of Christ. A damsel says to this bold Peter: "Thou also wast with this Jesus of Galilee." But he denied before them all, saying, "I know not what thou sayest." And when he was gone out into the porch another maid saw him and said unto them that were there, "This fellow was also with Jesus of Nazareth." And again he denied with an oath. "I do not know the Man." Another hour passed; and yet he did not realize his position; when another confidently affirmed that that he was a Galilean, for his speech betrayed him. And he was angry and began to curse and to swear, and again denied his Master: and the cock crew. (Matt. xxvi. 69–74.)

He commences away up on the pinacle of self-conceit, and goes down step by step until he breaks out into cursing, and swears that he never knew his Lord.

The Master might have turned and said to him, "Is it true, Peter, that you have forgotten Me so soon? Do you not remember when your wife's mother lay sick of a fever that I rebuked the disease and it left her? Do you not call to mind your astonishment at the draught of fishes so that you exclaimed, 'Depart from me; for I am a sinful man, O Lord?' Do you remember when in answer to your cry, 'Lord, save me, or I perish,' I stretched out My hand and kept you from drowning in the water? Have you forgotten when, on the Mount of Transfiguration, with James and John, you said to Me, 'Lord, it is good to be here: let us make three tabernacles?' Have you forgotten being with Me at the supper-table, and in Gethsemane? Is it true that you have forgotten Me so soon? The Lord might have upbraided him with questions such as these: but He did nothing of the kind. He cast one look on Peter: and there was so much love in it that it broke that bold disciple's heart: and he went out and wept bitterly.

And after Christ rose from the dead see how tenderly He dealt with the erring disciple. The angel at the sepulchre says, "Tell His disciples, *and Peter.*" (Mark xvi. 7.) The Lord did not forget Peter, though Peter had denied Him thrice; so He caused this kindly special message to be conveyed to the repentant disciple. What a tender and loving Saviour we have!

Friend, if you are one of the wanderers, let the loving look of the Master win you back; and let Him restore you to the joy of His salvation.

Before closing, let me say that I trust God will restore some backslider reading these pages, who may in the future become a useful member of society and a bright ornament of the Church. We should never have had the thirty-second Psalm if David had not been restored: "Blessed is he whose transgression is forgiven, whose sin is covered"; or that beautiful fifty-first Psalm which was written by the restored backslider. Nor should we have had that wonderful sermon on the day of Pentecost when three thousand were converted —preached by another restored backslider.

May God restore other backsliders and make them a thousand times more used for His glory than they ever were before.